# JEAN RHYS

List of author's previously published work:

*Love, Mystery and Misery: Feeling in Gothic Fiction*

*Private and Fictional Words: Canadian Women Novelists of the 1970s and 80s*

# JEAN RHYS

CORAL ANN HOWELLS

*Reader in Canadian Literature*
*University of Reading*

Harvester Wheatsheaf

New York London Toronto Sydney Tokyo Singapore

First published 1991 by
Harvester Wheatsheaf
66 Wood Lane End, Hemel Hempstead,
Hertfordshire, HP2 4RG
A division of
Simon & Schuster International Group

Typeset in 10/12pt Palatino by Witwell Ltd, Southport

Printed and bound in Great Britain

British Library Cataloguing in Publication Data

Howells, Coral Ann
Jean Rhys. – (Key women writers)
I. Title II. Series
823

ISBN 0-7108-1220-5
ISBN 0-7108-1221-3 pbk

1 2 3 4 5 95 94 93 92 91

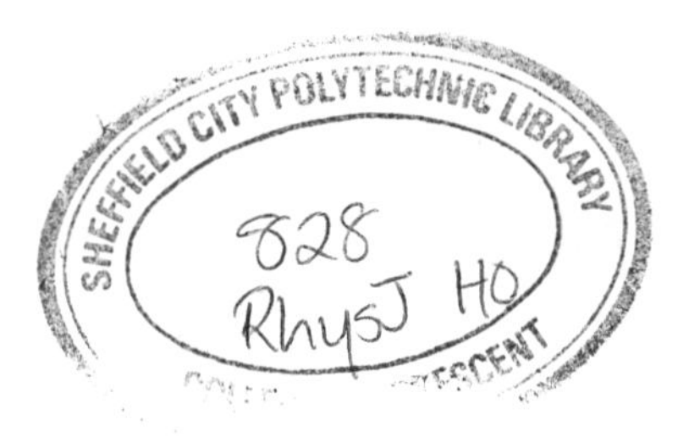

For Phoebe and Miranda, again

# *Titles in the Key Women Writers Series*

| | |
|---|---|
| Gillian Beer | *George Eliot* |
| Paula Bennett | *Emily Dickinson* |
| Penny Boumelha | *Charlotte Brontë* |
| Stevie Davies | *Emily Brontë* |
| Rachel Blau DuPlessis | *H.D.* |
| Kate Fullbrook | *Katherine Mansfield* |
| Jane Heath | *Simone de Beauvoir* |
| Coral Ann Howells | *Jean Rhys* |
| Deborah Johnson | *Iris Murdoch* |
| Angela Leighton | *Elizabeth Barrett Browning* |

# *Key Women Writers*

The *Key Women Writers* series has developed in a spirit of challenge, exploration and interrogation. Looking again at the work of women writers with established places in the main-stream of the literary tradition, the series asks, in what way can such writers be regarded as feminist? Does their status as canonical writers ignore the notion that there are ways of writing and thinking which are specific to women? Or is it the case that such writers have integrated within their writing a feminist perspective which so subtly maintains its place that these are writers who have, hitherto, been largely misread?

In answering these questions, each volume in the series is attentive to aspects of composition such as style and voice, as well as to the ideas and issues to emerge out of women's writing practice. For while recent developments in literary and feminist theory have played a significant part in the creation of the series, feminist theory represents no specific methodology, but rather an opportunity to broaden our range of responses to the issues of history, psychology and gender which have always engaged women writers. A new and creative dynamics between a woman critic and her female subject has been made possible by recent developments in feminist theory, and the series seeks to reflect the important critical insights which have emerged out of this new, essentially feminist, style of engagement.

It is not always the case that literary theory can be directly transposed from its sources in other disciplines to the practice of reading writing by women. The series investigates the possibility that a distinction may need to be made between feminist politics and the literary criticism of women's writing which has not, up to now, been sufficiently emphasised. Feminist reading, as well as feminist writing, still needs to be constantly interpreted and reinterpreted. The complexity and range of choice implicit in this procedure are represented throughout the series. As works of criticism, all the volumes in the series represent wide-ranging and creative styles of discourse, seeking at all times to express the particular resonances and perspectives of individual women writers.

*Sue Roe*

By a flicker in Mrs Sawyer's eyes I knew that worse than men who wrote books were women who wrote books – infinitely worse.

('The Day They Burned the Books')

Sometimes it was as if I were back there and as if England were a dream. Other times England was the real thing and out there was the dream, but I could never fit them together.

(*Voyage in the Dark*)

I know that to write as well as I can is my truth and why I was born, though the Lord knows I wish I hadn't been!

(*Letters*, 1959)

*Meek*!!! When I long to slaughter for a week or more. All over the place.

(*Letters*, 1959)

# Contents

# *Acknowledgements*

Perhaps the keenest pleasure in writing a book is the pleasure of discovery, and in this connection I would like to express my thanks to Sidney F. Huttner, Curator of Special Collections at the McFarlin Library, University of Tulsa, Oklahoma, and to Lori Curtis, the Assistant Curator, for so generously making available to me the riches of the Jean Rhys Collection. I am deeply grateful to them and to the Jean Rhys Estate for permission to quote so amply from that unpublished material, and to the British Academy for the Research Grant which made my visit possible. My warmest thanks to Dolores and Paul Brooks for their hospitality to me while I was a visitor to Tulsa. I would like to thank Donald Simpson, former Librarian of the Royal Commonwealth Society for opening the resources of that library to me, and I am grateful also for the resources of the Department of Manuscripts in the British Library and the University of London Library in Senate House.

I guess most books develop through frequent conversations and discussions, and this one seems to be filled with the echoes of other voices. I would like to thank Gillian Tindall, Anna Rutherford, Susheila Nasta and Rita Aldridge for early encouragement; Bonnie Kime Scott, Susan Merrill Squier and Lionel

Kelly for their helpful comments on modernism; John Thieme for stimulating discussions on colonialism and post-colonialism; Helen Stoddart for her perceptive remarks on the Gothic and on feminist theory, and Ruthina Newton who so enthusiastically shared with me her knowledge of her native Dominica.

My thanks to Carole Angier for directing me to Rhys manuscript materials in the British Library; to Annie Escuret and Paule Plouvier of the Université Paul Valery in Montpellier, and to my husband Robin Howells for their assistance in identifying some of Rhys's French literary models. I am grateful to Sue Roe, who out of her expert knowledge of Rhys has given me much-needed sensitive encouragement, and to Jackie Jones for her patience as editor during this project.

My thanks, as always, to my husband and to my daughters, Phoebe and Miranda, for their unfailingly loving support.

I have also to thank Andre Deutsch Ltd. for permission to reprint extracts from the following: *Quartet* by Jean Rhys. Published by Andre Deutsch Ltd., 1969. Copyright Jean Rhys 1928. *After Leaving Mr Mackenzie* by Jean Rhys. Published by Andre Deutsch Ltd., 1969. Copyright Jean Rhys 1930. *Voyage in the Dark* by Jean Rhys. Published by Andre Deutsch Ltd., 1967. Reprinted by permission of the Estate of Jean Rhys. It is believed that U.S. copyright has reverted to the author and was not renewed following the author's death. All reasonable attempts have been made to trace the copyright holder prior to publication. *Good Morning, Midnight* by Jean Rhys. Published by Andre Deutsch Ltd., 1967. Copyright Jean Rhys 1957. *Wide Sargasso Sea* by Jean Rhys. Published by Andre Deutsch Ltd., 1966. Copyright Jean Rhys 1966. *Tigers Are Better Looking* by Jean Rhys. Published by Andre Deutsch Ltd., 1968. Copyright Jean Rhys 1960, 1962, 1963, 1966, 1967. *Sleep It Off Lady* by Jean Rhys. Published by Andre Deutsch Ltd., 1976. Copyright the Estate of Jean Rhys 1976. *Jean Rhys Letters, 1931-1966*. Selected and edited by Francis Wyndham and Diana Melly. Published by Andre Deutsch Ltd., 1984. Copyright 1984, Selection, Francis Wyndham and Diana Melly. Copyright 1984, Introduction, Francis Wyndham. Copyright 1984, Letters, the Estate of Jean Rhys. *Smile Please* by Jean Rhys. Published by Andre Deutsch Ltd., 1979. Copyright the Estate of Jean Rhys 1979. Reprinted by permission of Andre Deutsch Ltd. and

HarperCollins Publishers. For permission to quote from unpublished manuscript materials the author is grateful to the following: the Jean Rhys Estate; Jean Rhys Collection, Department of Special Collections, Mc Farlin Library, University of Tulsa, Oklahoma; and the British Library.

# *Abbreviations*

Publication details can be found in the notes and bibliography.

| | |
|---|---|
| *ALMM* | *After Leaving Mr Mackenzie* |
| BEB | Black Exercise Book, held in the Jean Rhys Collection in the Department of Special Collections, McFarlin Library, University of Tulsa, Oklahoma |
| *GMM* | *Good Morning, Midnight* |
| *JRL* | *Jean Rhys : Letters, 1931-1966*, edited Francis Wyndham and Diana Melly |
| *LB* | *The Left Bank and Other Stories* |
| *PMS* | *Penguin Modern Stories* |
| *Q* | *Quartet* |
| *SIOL* | *Sleep It Off Lady* |
| *SP* | *Smile Please* |
| *TABL* | *Tigers are Better-Looking* |
| *VID* | *Voyage in the Dark* |
| *WSS* | *Wide Sargasso Sea* |

# *Introduction*

Jean Rhys's career may be read as a cautionary tale about the difficulties and dangers of a woman writing. As a white Creole girl from the small Caribbean island of Dominica she came to England in 1907 at the age of sixteen and lived as an expatriate in England and Europe till her death in 1979. She began writing in Paris in the 1920s under the patronage of Ford Madox Ford, and four of her five novels and one short story collection were published during the high modernist period of the 1920s and 30s. She then disappeared and her fiction went out of print. Only in the 1960s did her literary resurrection occur, and *Wide Sargasso Sea*, her best known novel and the one from which most readers gain their first impressions, was published in 1966 when she was seventy-six. That pattern of publication, disappearance and reissue of her fiction all within her own lifetime offers an emblematic account of what not infrequently happens to a woman writer's work and reputation after she is dead. The Rhys narrative containing the legend of her death and resurrection, to which she returns in her letters time and again with rueful glee ('so tactless of me to be still alive'), relates her personal case to a more general one. We are still celebrating her resurrection with the increasing attention being paid to her work, which is now seen as politically charged both in terms of the power politics of gender and the power politics of colonialism.

At the centre of our attention is the alienated Rhys heroine, but how do we 'read' this condition of alienation as Rhys describes it, and how do we identify Rhys's distinctive version of the feminine constructed in fiction that stretches – with a gap – over forty years? These are the questions I shall try to answer by reading Rhys through a critical framework which pays attention to the three intermeshing elements by which her writing was determined: the elements of gender, colonialism and modernism. In order to put together this version of the Rhys narrative, I have drawn on the insights of contemporary feminist theory, theories of colonial and post-colonial discourse, and revisionist studies of modernism which take gender into account.[1] The choice of such a multidimensional approach where three different perspectives all offer themselves as possible ways into reading Rhys is itself a comment on her fiction, just as it reflects the diversity of current critical attitudes to it.

Rhys's critics are of very different persuasions, highlighting very different aspects of her work.[2] The first three books on Rhys, all written at the end of her lifetime, lay out between them the directions that all subsequent criticism has taken. Louis James's *Jean Rhys*[3] unambiguously situated her as a novelist within the developing tradition of Caribbean writing and read her life as that of a colonial exile in Europe. James was following signposts already marked out by Caribbean critics like Wally Look Lai, V.S.Naipaul and John Hearne, all of whom saw *Wide Sargasso Sea* as an 'audacious metaphor' for the West Indian predicament with its tragic inheritance of colonialism.[4]

If, however, more attention was paid to her European novels, the Rhys narrative might be read very differently, as it was by Thomas F.Staley[5] (who incidentally was the first critic to make use of the Jean Rhys Collection at the University of Tulsa, to which only a preliminary catalogue was available at that stage). The focus of Staley's study was Rhys's female aesthetic, and, like the reviewers of the 1930s, he privileges the view of the Rhys heroine as passive victim. As a male critic, Staley appears to subscribe to traditionalist views of women as emotional, apolitical and helpless, and it seems that this attitude allows him, in common with Rhys's male protagonists, to be seduced by her women's images of dependence. Yet it must be said that Staley offers the first sustained criticism of her distinctive narrative techniques, astutely identifying both her relatedness to the modernist tradition and the kind of complicity between reader and text which her fictions solicit:

> Between the concentrated interiority of the text and the novel's brittle surface emerges a vision and a consistent tension which forms the basis for deep engagement between the reader and the work of art . . . The process for the reader becomes more a sense of shared discovery as the implications of the plot and narrative are embraced through a spatial, thematic and formal ordering, thus affording an aesthetic whole and creating a far richer potential text for the reader.[6]

Staley's views were challenged by Rhys's first feminist critic, Helen Nebeker,[7] who resists the reductiveness of a composite 'Rhys heroine' arguing instead for an archetypal reading centred on female myths and focused through Freudian and Jungian psychoanalytic models. While Nebeker locates the significance of Rhys's fiction in its portrayal of the obscured realities of women's experience, she has no clear feminist methodology nor does she write out of a coherent ideological framework. Her failure to recognise Rhys's colonial status, for example, leads her to misappropriate Rhys's sympathies in *Wide Sargasso Sea*:

> In Brontë's Jane is Rhys's almost archetypal woman–woman independent, freed from internal, cultural, economic pressures, so that she stands complete, psychically whole, absolutely in control of that feminine reality which is hers uniquely (symbolically, all that is ascribed to the realm of the unconscious).[8]

Later critics like Gayatri Spivak and Helen Tiffin have identified Rhys's position as the opposite of this in their discussions of *Wide Sargasso Sea* as 'post-colonial counterdiscourse'[9] and Teresa F. O'Connor[10] presents the subtlest study to date of the West Indian elements in Rhys's two novels that deal explicitly with Dominican experience, *Voyage in the Dark* and *Wide Sargasso Sea*. O'Connor's achievement lies in her linkage of the colonial vision of alienation with the theme of gender in Rhys's personal mythology 'that unites the experiences of the child, the woman, and the colonial in one voice'.[11]

It is a disadvantage that O'Connor's attention is so directed to the autobiographical elements in Rhys that she avoids or treats obliquely what might be seen as the central issue in Rhys's fiction: the challenge of constructing a female speaking subjectivity for her heroines. That challenge is taken up by Nancy R. Harrison and Deborah Kelly Kloepfer, both of whom explore Rhys's feminist poetics while relegating Caribbean elements to the subtext.[12] Harrison's interest in the rhetorical situation of twentieth century women writers leads her to focus, in her scrupulously detailed analysis of Rhys's writing practice, on what she calls the 'emphatic subjectivity' of Rhys's narratives:

> Rhys's 'unprecedented' world is a world of women's speech, of women talking back, saying what they want to say, in the interstices of the 'real' dialogue. It is this presentation, integral to the basic technical achievement of the novels, for which Rhys sets the precedent. It matters not if what her heroine-narrators want to say is unsuitable for today's more 'liberated' woman: the recording of a woman's unspoken responses within the set framework of masculine speech or discourse is the point.[13]

Where Harrison and Kloepfer differ is not over the question of Rhys's female speaking subjects, but over what the subject speaks. Whereas for Harrison it is a speaking back to a dominant masculine idiom, for Kloepfer it is a speaking back to the voices of absent mother figures. Unlike many feminist studies on women and language, Kloepfer does not locate women's difficultes exclusively in relation to patriarchal discourse, but shifts emphasis to the suppressed mother languages within women's texts and to Rhys's investigation of a feminine economy of loss in her stories of women's pain and silencing.

Kloepfer's book might be read as a valuable contribution to the study of modernist women's writing with its centring on daughters' relations to mothers rather than to fathers in an interesting reversal of traditional anxieties of influence. Her study of female modernist aesthetics is rather more accommodating of Rhys than the social and literary documentaries of Shari Benstock's *Women of the Left Bank: Paris 1900–1940*[14] and Sandra Gilbert and Susan Gubar's *No Man's Land: The Place of the Woman Writer in the Twentieth Century.*[15] In these massive feminist revisionist studies Rhys is no more than a marginal figure, but there are simple explanations for this. Though she lived in Paris in the 1920s she did not belong to the social network of American and British expatriate women writers and artists in Paris, so that she is not a substantial presence in Benstock's narrative about the 'feminine' identity of the Left Bank, and only her late 1930s novel *Good Morning, Midnight* figures at all. Nor does Rhys's fiction fit easily into Gilbert and Gubar's argument about the 'transformative nature of feminism' and she is mentioned only once. Rhys was a modernist writer by any criterion, and Bonnie Kime Scott's splendid anthology *The Gender of Modernism*[16] does manage to accommodate Rhys's complicitous critique of sexual and cultural politics within a more heterogeneous narrative about the female modernist condition.

Arguably these different perspectives highlight important issues of subjectivity not only within the fictions themselves but within the area of critical response. In what sense is Rhys's fiction so multiple, so secretive, that it constitutes a kind of blankness on to which critics can project their own ideological interests? In what sense are the fictions, like Rhys's heroines, at the mercy of their interpreters, objects of the gaze and transformed by that gaze, though themselves remaining other and always elusive? It seems that by a curious paradox Rhys's silenced heroines have been given multiple voices to state their condition of marginality and dispossession by Rhys's critics, though of course we need to put this proposition the other way around. Rhys's texts are themselves the site of these multiple voices which the critics hear and interpret through their different ideological frameworks.

What Rhys constructs through her fiction is, I would argue, a feminine colonial sensibility becoming aware of itself in a modernist European context, where a sense of colonial dispossession and displacement is focused on and translated into gendered terms, so that all these conditions coalesce, transformed into her particular version of feminine pain. Her texts are all versions of a fragmented female subjectivity, as

Rhys shows her heroines trying to construct an identity for themselves in radically unstable situations where traditions and social conventions prescribe certain rituals but are emptied of meaning. In this Waste Land, the discourse of her silenced protagonists is the field of multiple and contradictory voices: the voices of others through which the Rhys heroine has allowed her self-image to be constituted, and the insistent interruptions to these authoritative voices by her resistant inner voice which speaks out of secret knowledge of her own difference. Though about betrayal, disablement and the dispersal of identity, these are frequently fictions of precarious survival. Not surprisingly, the question with Rhys becomes a literary one: the survival of the fragmented woman as text, with fiction providing the only space where her dissident voice may be heard.

# Chapter One

# L'Etrangère

## I *Jean Rhys as a Woman Writer*

To read Rhys's statements about her writing is to come face to face with contradictions, most strikingly in her relation to the vocation of writing itself and on the connections between autobiography and fiction. Her response to her rediscovery in 1949 by Selma Vaz Dias (not the famous rediscovery of 1957 but the abortive one, when Vaz Dias first advertised in the *New Statesman* for permission to adapt *Good Morning, Midnight* for radio) reads like a compulsion to finish a life sentence:

> Now I'm really hanging on to my belief in fate – I never wanted to write. I wished to be happy and peaceful and obscure.
> I was *dragged* into writing by a series of coincidences – Mrs Adam, Ford, Paris – the need for money.
> I tried to stop – again I've been dragged back.
> So I must go on now failure or not – lies or no lies.[1]

The story of Rhys's writing career forges links between sentencing and sentences where the sentence becomes the means of life, power and self-validation:

> Why? Why? Why?

writing my life will have been an abject
to other people. But it could be an abject
ot have earned death.[2]

lictions are evident in her comments
here she alternates between seeing
inspiration with herself as passive
...neone's hand'[3] – and at other times
... herself as conscious fabricator. There is a mass of evidence, in her unpublished short story drafts and in her correspondence, documenting her meticulous revisions of *Wide Sargasso Sea* which illumines Rhys's writing practice, showing how she shifts around blocks of narrative, changes focalisations, always 'cutting to the bone' in her attempt to achieve something which is 'true as writing'. In an interview with Elizabeth Vreeland she spoke about the necessary transformations of fiction:

> The things you remember have no form. When you write about them, you have to give them a beginning, a middle and an end. To give life *Shape* – this is what a writer does. This is what is so difficult.[4]

We may wonder what is going on here. Is it personal mythmaking about her vocation, or a conscious adoption of disguises to preserve her secret self, or perhaps a genuine double voicing where both elements of these contradictory statements are true? Rhys speaks as a romantic who is a professional writer; she also speaks as a woman for whom writing is strongly associated with a sense of transgression against traditional notions of feminine decorum and a defiance of masculine authority. To present her writing as a curiously involuntary process related either to inspiration or to therapy is a way of evading full responsibility for her fictions of radical protest at the same time as preserving her image of feminine dependence.

Throughout her life Rhys was convinced that women who wrote books were the focus for a general contempt which transcended the hostilities of gender, class and culture. There are very few women writers in her fiction, and all of them are discredited or vilified. There is Sasha Jansen in *Good Morning, Midnight* ghost-writing fairytales for a rich woman in Antibes as a form of literary prostitution, and there are two nightmare images in the later stories: Mrs Lotus Heath in 'The Lotus', the woman writer stripped naked and running down the street pursued by the police in the middle of the night, and Laura in the war story 'I Spy a Stranger' who only invents titles for books but who is condemned as mad. Her list of titles suggests why such explosive potential needs to be contained and silenced by society:

> Titles of books to be written ten years hence, or twenty, or forty, or a hundred: *Woman as Obstacle to the Insect Civilisation? The Standardization of Woman, Misogyny* – well, call it misogyny – *Misogyny and British Humour* will write itself . . . *Misogyny and War, The Misery of Woman and the Evil in Men or the Great Revenge that Makes all the other Revenges Look Silly.* My titles go all the way from the sublime to the ridiculous.[5]

The terrifying images coalesce with Rhys's own paranoid sense in her old age of being regarded as a witch by the villagers in Cheriton Fitz Paine in Devon:

> It's the atmosphere of Cheriton Fitz, and its really unbelievable inhabitants . . . I'm disapproved or worse of because *I try to write* (!!) Well I resent this deeply and bitterly – how deeply no one knows but myself – and of course it is doing me great great harm.(*JRL*, p.240)

Being a witch harks back to being bewitched as punishment for reading (let alone writing) as a child in Dominica where her black nurse Meta terrified her: 'If you all read so much, you know what will happen to you? Your eyes will drop out and they will look at you from the page' (*SP*, p.28). Meta's female disapproval of an alien/alienating cultural pursuit is echoed by Mrs Sawyer's hatred of books and women writers in particular in 'The Day They Burned the Books', and interestingly it occupies the same chapter as the one which registers the girl child's awareness of literary discourse as patriarchal territory: 'Before I could read, almost a baby, I imagined that God, this strange thing or person I heard about, was a book' (*SP*, p.27). Not only the Bible, but the Encyclopaedia Britannica, history books, Milton's and Byron's poems, and novels, belong inside her father's bookcase. She has free access to them all, but the sense of transgression is there I believe, transferred to Meta's disapproval. It is only poetic discourse which is legitimated for her by her enthusiastic female teacher Mother Mount Calvary, 'I date all my love of words, especially beautiful words, to her half-ironical lessons' (*SP*, p.60). Significantly , it is poetry that the young Jean Rhys begins to write, as she told Francis Wyndham years later when working on *Wide Sargasso Sea*:

> I was rather down with this and that, so flew to writing poems. This I've always done (aged 12 or 10 when I started). They are strewn all over the places I've lived in – didn't keep many. I like some of them and can do them quickly.[6]

To Rhys writing was a private activity to be kept hidden, so that any attempt to publish was to put the secret self at risk. Though the unpublished drafts and notebooks flesh out the story of her writing career as a much more sustained and conscious process than she ever acknowledges in print, there remains her curious diffidence about assuming an authoritative voice and a hypersensitivity to criticism – not of her published work but of herself as a published writer. Her letters and the Black Exercise Book are strewn with savage comments on the attitude of the establishment, which she sees as Anglo-Saxon and male, towards women writers:

> I think that the anglo-saxon idea that you can be rude with impunity to any female who has written a book is utterly *damnable*. You come and have a look out of curiosity and then allow the freak to see what you think of her. It's only done of course to the more or less unsuccessful and only by anglo-saxons. (*JRL*, p.32)

Given these attitudes, Rhys was very much alive to the irony of her literary resurrection:

> I am very astonished that the BBC like my work (especially *Good Morning, Midnight*) but it seems they thought I was dead – which of course would make a great difference. In fact they were going to follow up with a broadcast, 'Quest for Jean Rhys' and I feel rather tactless being still alive!
> However I'm cheered up too for if they can make a fuss of me dead surely they can make a *little fuss* though I'm not. (*JRL*, p.61)

However, Rhys had to wait another eight years before the 'little fuss' began to turn to fame, with Deutsch finally managing to get in touch with her in 1957, and with the substantial support of Diana Athill and Francis Wyndham which resulted in the publication of *Wide Sargasso Sea* in 1966 and the reissue of all her novels by Deutsch between 1967 and 1969.

Rhys's personal sense of marginality and exclusion is written into her fictional narratives, which all focus on negative aspects of women's experience and female fantasy and on their exclusion from discourses of power and authority. The women she writes about are those on the precarious margins of respectability, or those who are sinking out of sight into drunkenness, prostitution or madness – silenced women whose angry protests at social and sexual injustice are always muted and self-destructive. The very features that make for the distinctiveness of Rhys's fiction are the ones likely to cause most problems for women readers, for while she exposes the hidden dynamics within social discourses of sexuality and power, her female protagonists never manage (never wish?) to evade those traditional structures or to unsettle the bastions of male power.

Her fiction raises the question, 'Are Women's Novels Feminist Novels?'[7] Rhys herself denied any feminist label, and on the face of it it is difficult to argue for the political consciousness of a writer who seems to derive her literary identity from the male symbolic code. 'Jean Rhys' was a pseudonym adopted at the time of her literary debut in Paris as Ford's protegée (though there had already been slippages from her given name, Ella Rees Williams, during her time as a chorus girl in the north of England). The two parts of the name are taken from her first husband's and her father's names, though we should note the subtle changes: 'Jean' could be masculine or feminine, and the spelling of 'Rhys' is changed from 'Rees', so that her literary name could be read as her adoption of the mantle of male protection whilst insisting on her individuation beneath such camouflage. The doubleness of her naming should alert us to Rhys's devious discourse in her fictions and her unfinished autobiography, for it is full of secrets and silences which use traditional female strategies of evasion to preserve the decorums of femininity while at the same time making space within those conventions for the expression of feelings traditionally forbidden to women.

Yet it would not be possible to read Rhys's fiction as a simple statement of gender ideology about the oppression of women by patriarchal society, not only because she reveals sexual power politics to be a system of mutual exploitation, but most significantly because sexual politics are imbricated in a wider system of social power relationships. Within that discourse gender is only one factor, for class and money are equally imperious, and in Rhys's particular case so is her colonial construct of Englishness. Her fiction is multivoiced discourse where the voices of tradition crisscross and echo against the voices of contemporary inheritors, spelling out one woman's problematic relation to her double cultural heritage.

As a series of fragmented commentaries on the traditional discourse of sexual power politics, Rhys's novels engage in recognisably feminist dialogue, speaking back to the patriarchal order in a way that resembles Luce Irigaray's feminist critique of Freud.[8] In *Speculum de l'autre femme* (1974) Irigaray speaks back to Freud's 1933 essay on 'Femininity', and by a curious coincidence, Rhys had already spoken back to that essay in the 1930s, as I shall discuss in my treatment of the 'Mr Howard story' later in this section. Indeed, in her deliberately non-theoretical way Rhys explores the same territory that contemporary feminist theorists have arrived at fifty years later. Through her stories of doomed dissenting women, she exposes the interests at stake in male centred psychoanalytic constructs of the feminine, just as she explores collaborative sexual fantasies where women are perceived and perceive themselves as objects of the male gaze. Not only does her fiction represent women's attempts at intervention into patriarchal discourse, but this is itself a form of *écriture feminine* in her use of 'mother languages' and her writing of the female body as, quite literally, 'le corps souffrant'. She offers alternative versions to traditional stories of patriarchy and imperialism which are ignored or unheard within the fictions themselves because they are unspoken, for as Rhys shows, her female protagonists are silenced by the very orders of that discourse. These are all stories about women's failure to articulate their resistant view. In ways that are again very similar to Irigaray's encounter with

Freud's master text on woman, Rhys questions patriarchal pronouncements, though her fictions still bespeak a collusion with the principle of male authority so that her challenge is often closer to seduction than to rebellion.

The double bind repeatedly rehearsed in her fictions is that despite their awareness of the social structures within which they are trapped, her heroines do not attempt to break out; instead they assiduously try to stay within the conditions of their entrapment, where every new instance of betrayal represents another expulsion from paradise. Though her fictions offer a merciless exposure of a female predicament, women's resistance to the metanarrative of male imperialism is undermined by their being caught in a 'movement between complicity and critique', as Rachel Blau Du Plessis describes the dilemma of modernist women writers.[9] These fictions do not offer solutions to women's dilemmas, but they are radical investigations of the social and psychological constructions of gender as Rhys writes in suppressed female narratives which deconstruct ready-made definitions of Woman in favour of representations of individual women. It is in this invention of a dialogue situation that her fictions are so innovatory: 'I seem to be brought up willy-nilly against the two sides of the question. Sometimes I ask myself if I am the only one who is; for after all, who knows or cares if there are two sides?' (*SP*, p.64)

Rhys's fiction is full of chorus girls, kept women, prostitutes and finally the mad Creole wife, also the figures of mannequins, mirrors, masks and puppets, as her protagonists allow their self-images to be imposed from outside. There is an obsessive attention to codes of dress and manners, and to girls' education, which is shown to be a decisive agent in the process of gender construction, leaving them vulnerable and unprepared for the risks of adult life. In her depiction of these stereotype roles as male fantasy objects, Rhys shows how it is that women are deprived of authority over their own lives and how they are forced into a position of manipulative dependence. Her heroines all spend long periods alone in single rooms, usually paid for by men, waiting for men. In such situations, Rhys's women are engaged in drinking too much or sleeping, reconstructing themselves as the blanks which patriarchal society insists that they be, and trying to forget. (Of herself Rhys wrote, 'I became very good at blotting things out, refusing to think about them' (*SP*. p.62)

The painful areas which these women refuse to explore but which hover on the edges of consciousness or surface in dreams, relate to the personal and social histories through which and against which their sense of themselves as gendered subjects has been constituted. These historical dimensions carry such a freight of pain that they are suppressed by the consciousness, but they are there as evidence of the subtext to the scripted self; these are the voices which speak the doubleness and fragmentation experienced by Rhys's female subjects.

I would like to return to the issue of women's complicity in patriarchal discourses of sexuality and power, which for women take the form of romantic fantasies of falling in love as a state of self-abandonment to male mastery. These fantasies are written into women's fiction from eighteenth-century Gothic novels to Mills and Boon and Harlequin romances, and indeed are scrutinised by many contemporary feminist critics and novelists.[10] Perhaps the most lucid formulation of this romantic thralldom is Canadian novelist Alice Munro's:

> Then I come back again and again to the center of my fantasy, to the moment when you give yourself up, give yourself over to the assault which is guaranteed to finish off everything you've been before. A stubborn virgin's belief, this belief in perfect mastery; any broken-down wife could tell you there is no such thing.[11]

While it is generally assumed that such fantasy narratives are culturally constructed and that women's education in romance is derived from social practices, books, films and popular songs, Rhys offers an extraordinary account of the origins of this female romantic fantasy in her own personal experience as an adolescent. In the Black Exercise Book she tells the story of her own en-gendering as a female subject and of the intensity of her imaginative engagement with a sexual narrative of love, cruelty and female submission, told to her by 'a handsome old Englishman of about 72 or 73' called Mr Howard. For Rhys this is not a narrative derived from books; it is a narrative given her by a man, in which she participates.[12]

It is worth looking closely at Rhys's account for what it

reveals about a personal dynamics of femininity and for its far-reaching implications in her fictional narratives. Rhys herself had no doubt of its crucial importance, for as she suggests in the preface to the Mr Howard story , 'I was just at this stage when it happened – the thing that formed me, made me as I am – the thing I want to write about.' (BEB). But the 'thing itself' is delayed for five-and-a-half pages while Rhys establishes in her typically associative way the context for the story. Indeed the process of her telling here is emblematic of her fictional methods, where her narratives are figured out more completely via image associations than through linear plot connections. She talks about her adolescent sense of slippage away from childhood certainties as she becomes aware of the ambiguities of her position as a white Creole, and she also mentions her childish inarticulateness when faced with her father's kindness. It is within this framework that she situates her conversations with Mr Howard, the family friend who showed an interest in her, taking her for walks in the park and paying her attention, in the process 'mentally seducing' her through his serial story about love and sex: 'A lover is tall and dark and beautiful and strong. A lover smiles at you and hurts you.' (BEB).

Rhys records how he once fondled her breasts, and then in the face of her confusion and fear bought her sweets, only to resume his narrative another day:

> Would you like to belong to me?
> I don't know I gasped breathlessly heart beating looking into the eyes.
> It was then that it began.
> I'd seldom allow you to wear clothes at all – what would happen afterwards
> The serial story to which I listened for was it weeks or months?
> one day he would abduct me and I'd belong to him and we went home in a dream . . .
> Always in the end punished – that is love – And only that. To give yourself up entirely hopelessly not for the fear of hell not for hope of heaven . . .
> After 2 or 3 doses of this drug because that's what it was I no longer struggled . . .
> But the terrible thing was the way something in the depths of me said, Yes, that is true: pain humiliation submission that is for me. It filled me with all I knew of life with all I'd ever felt. It fitted like a hook fits an eye. (BEB).

The Mr Howard narrative continues in fragments over about twelve pages of the Exercise Book, gathering into a loose continuum Rhys's comments on the charms of romantic narrative and her own complicity in their shared fantasy (for Mr Howard's serial story became a dialogue, prompted by the girl's questions about what she might wear and what they would eat), her remarks on the little Creole girl in *High Wind in Jamaica* and on the connections between sex, slavery, pain and death. The account curiously gathers to itself the dream of sexual fascination and dread that appears as Antoinette's in *Wide Sargasso Sea* which Rhys tells as belonging to her adolescence, a subconscious continuation of the Mr Howard story after his departure for England. This dream is followed by an account of her mother's rejection of her in favour of her little sister, and then the final entry on Mr Howard: 'He said, How white your hands are against the grass – He said, Let her naked be, teaching the sheets a whiter hue than white. He said, I wouldn't often let you wear clothes you understand.'

The Black Exercise Book is undated, but this amazingly uncensored account must have been written after Rhys had finished *Voyage in the Dark* and while writing *Good Morning, Midnight*, for she says that she is writing a novel about Paris and 'the last love adventure of a woman who is growing old.' The Mr Howard story meshes in with her creative writing process:

> It has relieved me to write. I wish I could get it clearer, this pain that has gone through all my life. However I've tried to escape it has reached out and brought me back.
> Now I don't try any longer. I felt in Paris that I was being possessed by something and I have given myself up to it this time unreservedly as utterly as in Mr Howard's story I had to give myself up to my imaginary lover . . . Was that what I've been always meant to learn? (BEB)

The positioning of the Mr Howard story makes it clear that this state of possession and total submission includes sex and the imaginative life of telling stories and writing novels. A hidden text written in the margins (in pencil in a notebook) and omitted from her autobiography, it pervades Rhys's own narrative of the creative life and her heroines' enslavement to romantic fantasies. The story surfaces only at the end of her career in 'Goodbye Marcus, Goodbye Rose' which was published in the *New Yorker* in 1976 and in her last collection, though this version has a more shapely ending than the notebook narrative. The brusque 'I forgot it' (BEB) is replaced by Phoebe's loss of innocence and her welcoming of prospects 'far more exciting.' (SIOL, p. 30)

Rhys never succeeded in burying or accommodating Mr Howard's serial story, 'a joke rare and curious this old boy was unloading on me. And I fool and was then fool. I lapped it up and asked for more.' (BEB) Fascinatingly she even sought for some explanation of the spell through psychoanalysis, and this was the occasion when, like Irigaray later, she encountered Freud's essay on 'Femininity'. In the Black Exercise Book she writes of her visit to Sylvia Beach's bookshop in Paris:

> I wanted a book on Psycho-analysis. I found one and this is the sense of what I read: 'Women of this type will invariably say that they were seduced when young by an elderly man. They will relate a detailed story which in every way is entirely fictitious. (BEB)[13]

Rhys comments:

> No honey I thought it is *not* fictitious in every case
> By no means and anyhow how do you know? (BEB)

She criticises 'this gentleman' for laying down the law about the female attitude and reactions to sex, 'Then I put the book down'. She continues:

> I wish that some time some place a man would write about women fairly. I suppose it's an impossible task. Some Frenchmen almost do it though. (BEB)

Like later feminist theorists, Rhys rejects male-centred psychoanalysis as reductive, though for slightly different reasons from Irigaray's; she asserts that the seduction experience was true in her own case and moreover that the mental seduction lasts forever: 'Life isn't like they tell you, even books on psychoanalysis.' (BEB)

Yet a psychoanalytical reading of the Mr Howard story adds an important dimension to our understanding of Rhys's women's relation to sexuality and desire; and Jane Gallop's discussions of Freud and Lacan as well as her chapter on Irigaray would seem to gloss some of its most significant elements.[14] In her complaint that neither Freud nor Lacan ever discussed the specificity of female sexuality, Gallop quotes from Ernest Jones's paper on 'The Early Development of Female Sexuality' (1927):

> There is a healthy suspicion growing that men analysts have been led to adopt an unduly phallo-centric view . . . the importance of the female organs being correspondingly underestimated.[15]

It is worth noting that in Rhys's version of her 'mental seduction' Mr Howard does not underestimate them; on the contrary he goes straight for the twelve-year-old girl's breasts, the physical sign of her sexual difference. In this seduction through language, the question we need to ask is, what is the relation of the female subject to the signifiers in Rhys's account? Rhys speaks plainly here of a girl's having her sexuality and her desire constructed through discourse, just as Mr Howard's desire is coded here as well, where his pleasure derives from his fantasy of cruelty. As Gallop remarks, the phallic role demands impassivity though the evidence of pleasure undermines the rigid authority of the paternal/patriarchal position.

One question remains: why did Rhys go to Sylvia Beach's bookshop in the first place? It appears that Rhys wanted to know exactly what Irigaray wanted to know:

> As for woman, *on peut se demander* [one could wonder, ask oneself] why she submits so easily . . . to the counterphobic projects, projections, productions of man relative to his desire'.[16]

Gallop's comment opens up vistas which Rhys refused to contemplate:

> The question of why woman complies must be asked. To ask that question is to ask what woman must not do anymore, what feminist strategy ought to be.[17]

With the proviso that 'the answer is not so obvious', Gallop does hazard, via her reading of Irigaray's reading of Freud, an answer to Rhys's question:

> The law of the father gives her an identity, even if it is not her own, even if it blots out her feminine specificity. To give it up is not a 'simple' matter. It must be done over and over.[18]

That comment brings us close to the centre of female romance and to the reasons for the irresolution of that fantasy of falling in love so endlessly re-enacted. Gallop's concluding remarks on Irigaray's encounter with Freud might have been made as comment on the Mr Howard story and its resonance in Rhys's fictions of feminine desire:

> Maybe what frightens her is not seduction of the father or by the father but 'making love'. 'Love' has always been sublimated, idealized desire, away from the bodily specificity . . . 'Love' is entangled with the question of woman's complicity: it may be the bribe which has persuaded her to agree to her own exclusion.[19]

'Sublimation', 'complicity' and 'exclusion' are the key words in Rhys's stories of women in love, where fantasies of innocence and protection mesh with fantasies of sexual dread and victimisation in ways that are reminiscent of earlier Gothic fiction. So it is not surprising to find that the situations and scenarios of traditional Gothic should reappear in these stories of women dying or being broken up; of women attempting to commit suicide or drinking themselves to death, trying to forget their insights and their hurts; of women deprived of their biological status and producing only abortions and dead babies, and finally of women deprived of their sanity. It is a dreadful catalogue of desperation and pain, with one possible ending which Rhys unambiguously achieves only after her 'resurrection' from nearly thirty years of silence: female revenge and self-destruction. The version of female Gothic Rhys offers is not the one that belongs to the contemporary revisionism of Margaret Atwood or Angela Carter, where the female victim complex is exposed as irresponsible and damaging fantasy. Instead, Rhys's novels present the female victim complex as a distinctive construct of the feminine, where Gothic fantasising becomes itself a mechanism of defence against reality.

These stories of women's entrapment do not revise the old female romantic fantasy narratives nor do they really effect, even in fiction, any shift in the traditional balance of power between the sexes. Women readers of Rhys are faced with the choice of being collaborative critics enjoying the pleasures and pains of recognition, or of being resisting readers or – a third possibility – of oscillating between these two positions as Judith Kegan Gardiner suggests.[20] Again it is a question of complicity, this time between reader and text, for Rhys's fiction belongs to the dangerous regions of women's fears and resistance and compromise. I suspect that in the end Rhys's appeal is fairly insidious. Though her novels may be read as offering a radical critique of sexual power politics, it could equally well be argued that in her retelling of romance plots which always end in women's betrayal and failure, she speaks to women's deepest insecurities, just as her stories of women's rage at social and sexual injustice and their silencing may be read as confirming women's deepest fears.

## II *Jean Rhys as a Colonial Writer*

> I thought, Am I an expatriate? Expatriate from where?
> ('Leaving School: How I Became a Novelist')[21]

Rhys's sense of being a misfit focuses a key issue relating to her position as a woman and as a colonial writer, for if otherness is the condition of woman, so displacement is 'the special post-colonial crisis of identity'.[22] Indeed, a word needs to be said about the terms 'colonial' and 'post-colonial' here. Historically, Rhys belongs to the period of Empire and her own formation as a white Creole is a distinctively colonial one; yet her subversive critique of Englishness and imperialism (focused by her recognition of difference after her arrival in England) should more appropriately be described as a post-colonial impulse. Her two West Indian novels might be seen as illustrating the shift from one position to the other, with *Voyage in the Dark* envisaging the colonial moment of total dereliction and *Wide Sargasso Sea* as a post-colonial statement of resistance to an imperialist text. It is a question of relationship to literary and cultural inheritances and of thinking beyond traditional cultural dependencies, in order to find a voice as a speaking subject. For Rhys the problems of situating herself as a subject are multiplied: within which cultural discourse does she belong, either at home in the Caribbean or in England, the mother country? It has been Rhys's fate to be regarded as an outsider in both cultures. In Europe she was perceived as definitely not English, by Ford in Paris in the 1920s and by Alec Waugh who met her in London in the 1930s: 'Dominica was a clue to her just as she was a clue to it'.[23] Yet, writing to Waugh from Dominica in 1949, Elma Napier asked, 'Incidentally, who is Jean Rhys? None of us have ever heard of her'.[24] As an expatriate living in Europe, Rhys was not recognised as a Caribbean writer till Wally Look Lai's groundbreaking essay on *Wide Sargasso Sea* in 1968.[25] Though contemporary critics of the New Literatures in English have affirmed her position within the Caribbean tradition, that position is still sufficiently ambiguous for critics who wish to focus on other aspects of her writing to blank out the issue of colonialism, and there are critics who do not see *Wide Sargasso Sea* as a representative Caribbean text.[26] Antoinette in that novel speaks for Rhys's personal crisis of identity when she asks the question, 'So between you I often wonder who I am and where is my country and where do I belong and why was I ever born at all?'[27]

Rhys explores the contradictions of the white Creole situation in the Caribbean at the end of the nineteenth century in her fiction and non-fiction, with perhaps her frankest statement in an unpublished entry in the Black Exercise Book:

> I was curious about black people. They stimulated me and I felt akin to them. It added to my sadness that I couldn't help but realise they didn't really like or trust white people – white cockroaches they called us. Sick with shame at some of the stories of the slave days . . . Yet all the time knowing that there was another side to it. Sometimes seeing myself powerful . . . sometimes being proud of my great grandfather, the estate, and the good old days, . . . But the end of my thinking about them was always a sick revolt and I wanted to be identified with the other side which of course was impossible.[28]

Her own family history encapsulates the latter stage in the history of the plantation system in the British Caribbean, for her mother's family the Lockharts had been plantation and slave owners in Dominica since the late eighteenth-century after that island had been captured from the French and annexed by Britain in 1763.[29] The fortunes of their family estate at Geneva, which still belonged in the family when Rhys was a child, reflected the traumatic dismantling of the plantation world that took place in the nineteenth century. Though Dominica with its small estates was never the site of large-scale slave unrest, there was a degree of local violence; the house at Geneva had been burned down several times and was again a ruin during Rhys's own lifetime, while economic instability characterised the nineteenth-century Caribbean colonies. Slavery was legally abolished in British possessions in 1838, but as Philip Curtin argues, formal legal emancipation creates a misconception in the modern mind, for many of the practices and assumptions of the plantation system with its privileging of white supremacy continued throughout the nineteenth century and into the twentieth. In Dominica, as in Jamaica, the old sugar estates suffered an economic decline, and Rhys was born into the last vestiges of that plantation society. Her father, a Welsh doctor, had married a Miss Lockhart and then acquired two small estates of his own, where he lived for the rest of his life. However, his second wife, an Englishwoman and Rhys's stepmother, sold them and returned to England after his death, and by then his children had already left. Ella (Jean Rhys) was sent to England in 1907 with her aunt to finish her education. She hated the Perse School for Girls in Cambridge where she was called 'West Indies', and left after a term to go to the Academy of Dramatic Art in London. She returned only once to Dominica: in 1936 with her second husband Leslie Tilden Smith, who drew a meticulous map of the island, recording as many details as he could of that forgotten family history. Little survived of the West Indian society of Rhys's youth: even the Imperial Road, aptly named as a monument of empire and the opening of which Rhys had attended as a child had vanished. (This is the same road that Alec Waugh described in the late 1940s through a masculine European frame of reference as 'worse than a duckboard track at Passchendale'.[30])

By the very facts of Caribbean colonial history, Rhys's inheritance was one of ruins, dispossession and estrangement in the country where she was born. *Smile Please* records her traumatic sense of rejection by the land itself, in feminised imagery through which she inscribes also her separation from her own mother:

> It was alive, I was sure of it. Behind the bright colours softness, the hills like clouds and the clouds like fantastic hills. There was something austere, sad, lost, all these things. I wanted to identify myself with it, to lose myself in it. (But it turned its head away, indifferent, and that broke my heart.) (*SP* p. 81)

Rhys was also a British subject, and her position in relation to England needs to be considered. Through her colonial education she was encouraged to construct an idealised model of Englishness, as the standard against which her own place and culture were measured. By definition within the discourse of imperialism, colonial culture was invariably found to be inferior – suffering either from lack or from excess.[31] Though Dominica's layered history of multiple European conquests and settlement from the seventeenth century onwards disturbs any simple imposition of British imperial discourse, the island had been a British colony since the end of the eighteenth century and the English language and English culture of the governing class was certainly privileged there at the turn of the century. Like many children all over the Empire whose image of England was constructed through books and pictures, Rhys fell under its spell:

> Coming in from these rides I always felt that life was glorious and would certainly become more so later on (England, England!). (*SP*, pp. 164–5)

The shock of coming face to face with the real thing is registered in *Smile Please* in one poignant sentence of transition. It is this sentence from which Diana Athill takes the title for the unfinished second part: 'Then, quite suddenly it seemed, it began to grow cold' (*SP* p. 97). Rhys continued to suffer from an alienated vision of England for the rest of her life, though never quite ridding herself of her colonial subject position:

> Always like a constant aching, no, an irritation, harsh, gritty, this feeling about England and the English. Disappointed love, of course. (*SP*, p. 165)

More frequently in her fiction this 'disappointed love' takes the form of covert and compromised resistance, though it does on occasions blaze out in furious satire against the imperialist stance, as on the opening pages of the Black Exercise Book:

> This dear country of ours which has attained its present envied position by the simple expedient of betraying all its friends one after the other and always for strictly moral reasons . . . You've got to do it with a straight face and honest eyes too. 'Honest eyes our speciality – Plat du jour – Boiled eyes served cold.' [Then she adds] This article will have to be rewritten. (BEB)

There is plenty of evidence of Rhys's Caribbean inheritance in her fiction, not only in *Voyage in the Dark* and *Wide Sargasso Sea* but in the short stories in all three of her collections as well as the late story 'Temps Perdi' where she makes explicit connections between the colonial mentality and gender relations. These multivoiced texts interweave the different discourses that co-exist within hybridised Caribbean culture. In their resistance to what Spivak calls 'imperialism and its territorial and subject-constituting project,' [32] these fictions adopt many of the strategies of colonial and post-colonial counter-discourse, insistently figuring internalised narratives of loss which run as subtexts to the main texts, disrupting the voices of authority in the narrative subject's attempts to reconstruct an identity that is already fragmented. *Wide Sargasso Sea* is the most rebellious of Rhys's counter-discourses, as it writes against the representation of white Creole woman in a female text which is also one of the classic texts of nineteenth-century British imperialism. Rhys's double rebellion signals the dimensions of her sense of outsiderliness, so that it is a fitting irony that this novel should be the text through which Rhys's literary resurrection was effected and on which her reputation in the English and the Caribbean literary traditions has been established.

## III *Jean Rhys as a Modernist Writer*

As Ford's protegée, Rhys's first short story 'Vienne' published in his *Transatlantic Review* in 1924 placed her name in a roll call of contributors to that short-lived periodical which reads like a Who's Who of expatriate modernist artists in Paris: Gertrude Stein, Djuna Barnes, Nancy Cunard, Mina Loy, Dorothy Richardson, Ernest Hemingway, Ezra Pound, Joseph Conrad, as well as Paul Valéry, Tristan Tzara and Picasso. Rhys's fiction belongs within the heterogeneous aesthetic of modernism, though critical recognition of her as a modernist writer has been long delayed. It is only now with the redefinitions of modernism, frequently under revisionary pressures of postmodernism and feminism, that its multiplicities – already signalled in those representative *Transatlantic Review* names – are becoming evident.[33] Crucially for Rhys, the deconstruction of the male modernist metanarrative has opened up spaces within which her feminine poetics of alienation and compromised resistance may be accommodated.[34] Her version of modernism encodes gender and colonial differences in the figure of the outsider who without money, power or social position launches her critique against the complacency of authority from the margins, while her fictions offer a subjectively focused perspective on distinctively modernist anxieties and obsessions.

Rhys herself was always socially on the margins of the Left Bank international set when she lived in Paris in the 1920s. Though there are good reasons why this might be so, relating to her economic circumstances, her being married and her colonial background, it is also worth remembering that she was no more disadvantaged than many other female expatriate writers and artists in Paris at the time. There is the distinct possibility that this was a deliberately chosen position of resistance against what she saw as an Anglo-American fantasy about European cosmopolitan living. In a letter written in the 1960s she reflects with characteristic malice on that expatriate society:

> I struck a book yesterday written about the nineteen twenties in Montparnasse. Not an Englishman. Very good. Very. Especially as he stressed something that no one here realises at all. The 'Paris' all these people write about, Henry Miller, even Hemingway etc was not 'Paris' at all – it was 'America in Paris' or 'England in Paris'. The real Paris had nothing to do with that lot – As soon as the tourists came the *real* Montparnos packed up and left . . . That is quite true. And if I saw something of the other Paris – it's only left me with a great longing which I'll never satisfy again. (*JRL*, p. 280)

While her contemporaries (apart from Ford) did not take a great deal of interest in Rhys or in her fiction, nor she in them, she did take an interest in their writing. The allusions to Joyce and Eliot in her novels and her remarks in letters and other unpublished writings reveal a much wider familiarity with modernist fiction and poetry than has previously been assumed. Her own bilingual education in Dominica had given her a knowledge of the French precursors of modernism like Flaubert and Maupassant, and under Ford's tutelage she embarked on an extensive reading programme in contemporary French literature. She was also familiar with the writings of her contemporaries in English, as her following outburst against 'thought control' in the 1950s suggests:

> Why say as Mr Green does, 'I demand a positive and creative view of life?' What is that? And why *demand* a view of life.
> Not his business surely.
> It's all very well to talk about 'The Old Man and the Sea' but what about 'Hills Like White Elephants' or 'A Way You'll Never Be' [or 'The Dead' I think it's called].[35]
> Would those be up to his 'positive and creative' standard?
> I do feel rather deeply about the thought control matter. So insidious. And suddenly it's there - Not to be resisted any more. (*JRL*, pp. 99–100)

Rhys's own writing, which would probably not meet Mr Green's demands any more than Hemingway's or Joyce's did, is also distinctively modernist in its aesthetic and its subject matter. Her European fiction of the 1920s and 30s is concerned with constructing a poetics of urban space, in a project similar to Joyce, Eliot, and Pound, or Mallarme and Baudelaire, but unlike them she does it from a feminised perspective.[36] Like *Ulysses* or *The Waste Land*, Rhys's fiction has a sense of isolation and psychic fragmentation, together with the multiple voices of male and female characters, the voices of memory and history, snatches of popular songs and literary allusions, interweaving past and present so that boundaries dissolve. However, in Rhys's female version of modernism there are no myths for reassurance, no fragments to shore against her ruins, for she is always referring to literary and cultural traditions from which as a woman she has been exiled. This necessitates a revision of male constructs of modernism, for Rhys's women are placed in the situation of modernist *flâneurs* who are disabled by their feminine conditioning from taking advantage of the metropolitan experience. Adrift on the streets of Paris, Vienna or London, they desire exactly the opposite of rootlessness and promiscuity; locked into their own romantic fantasies they are really much closer to Rapunzel in her tower, desiring rescue and protection rather than adventure. However, for them the only retreat is the single hotel room which spells shelter and privacy but also privation and imprisonment. Metropolitan spaces are masculine spaces, voided of meaning except of the most trivial kinds, or else perceived as actively hostile to women. The modernist urge for epiphanies, so often satisfied in male writing by glimpses into the city's secret life, is denied to Rhys's female protagonists. The possibility of meaning hovers for Marya, for Anna, for Julia or Sasha, but the city never organises itself into moments of revelation; on the contrary it is figured as a Gothic labyrinth or a futurist nightmare, always a place of female dread.

As a modernist voice, Rhys speaks from a self consciously marginal position, raising issues of gender and colonial difference in fictions of resistance which are always compromised by the conditions of female dependency. Her own condition as a woman adrift is beautifully evoked in this unpublished memory fragment written in the 1930s in London. As a sketch of Paris café life it registers the distinctive mixture of glamour, dislocation and angst which belonged to the 1920s. There is a personal subtext here, which carries echoes of Rhys's romantic and literary entanglement with Ford (for he is the 'friend') and of her own private love affair with Paris. Its surface delicately figures a fragmented sense of life as theatrical performance where human casualties are made invisible, where male voices call the tunes, and where the female subject occupies a position of irresponsibility and silence:

> I was homesick for Paris and thought about my last evening in Paris spent at the Lapin Agile [Fiedler's?] in Montmartre.
> His singer a white Russian had shot herself and a young man posed against black velvet curtains was reading Verlaine instead.
> Pour un coeur que j'ennuie
> Oh le chant de la pluie

There you are, said my friend. An omen. You'll go back to London. I thought, I've never heard the sound of the rain in London.[37]

# Chapter Two

# *Other Stories:* The Left Bank and Other Stories *and* Quartet

Jean Rhys's first two books provide a fascinating instance of a woman writing back to male authority, for there is no doubt that both of them encode her response to her relationship with Ford Madox Ford in the mid-1920s in Paris. They were written and published as a direct result of that relationship, where Ford began as her patron and literary mentor, and later became her lover. Rhys tells in *Smile Please* how her work was brought to Ford's attention, and it was he as editor of the *Transatlantic Review* who published her first story 'Vienne' in 1924. Situated as she was, an unknown and unpublished outsider, Ford's encouragement and masculine approval enabled her to assume a vocation which had only existed in rough draft up to the time of their meeting. Ford's coterie of expatriates in Paris operated within a different set of social and literary conventions from traditionalist expectations about women, and, though Rhys always remained on the periphery, Ford's professional help to her as an aspiring writer was invaluable.

Rhys gives a brief account of her writing apprenticeship with Ford in 'Leaving School: How I Became a Novelist':

> So began several months of writing short stories and having them

> torn to pieces or praised. 'Don't be so glib.' Dont do this. Do that. Or Don't take the slightest notice of what I say or what anybody says. 'About Triple Sec,' I said one day. 'Dont you like it at all?' 'Oh that. Put it away, dont think about it just now. Write another short story.' 'I dont want to,' I said, rather sulkily. 'Then translate one of my books into French. Its very good practice.' 'I dont know French well enough,' I said. 'Then try La Maison de Claudine into English. Bring me all you can do of the first chapter tomorrow.[1]

Rhys writes frankly about their professional relationship, and Ford, in addition to praising her writing in his Preface to her *Left Bank* stories, mentions her in one of his letters as the translator of Francis Carco's *Perversity*, attempting to set the record straight as the translation had been published under his name.[2] Neither of them, unsurprisingly, discusses their love affair outside fiction. Yet in important ways that double-faced relationship marks Rhys's narrative stance in her first two books, and these provide a fascinating instance of a woman writing back to male authority. Rhys assumes a very different position in *The Left Bank and Other Stories*, where she is writing back to Ford as literary mentor, from the one in *Quartet*, where she writes back to him as lover. Whereas the stories are multivoiced in their resistance and wittily subversive of Ford's Preface, *Quartet* is cast in traditional Gothic form as the obsessional narrative of a female victim, told almost entirely in a single voice. Marya's oscillation between savage criticism of Heidler and self-abnegation suggests a woman meshed into a psychic script about sexual power politics from which she cannot escape, and just as Marya's romantic fantasy cannot be worked out or progressed from, so her story is insistently rewritten, though not revised, in all Rhys's other novels. Some critics have claimed that Ford had already scripted the affair with Rhys in his fiction years before he met her.[3] With equal justification that privilege might be claimed for Rhys, for arguably it was her fantasy script (already written in the Mr Howard story) which coerced Ford into assuming, very temporarily, the hero-villain role in her life.

## The Left Bank and Other Stories[4]

It is an astonishing feature of Jean Rhys's first book *The Left Bank and Other Stories* that there is no story by Rhys called 'The Left Bank'; this refers to the Preface by Ford entitled 'Rive Gauche', so that Rhys is the writer of the 'Other Stories.' When we consider Ford's Preface and the fact that he occupies sixteen of its twenty pages in recounting his own experiences of the Left Bank, driving Jean Rhys to the margins at the end, we begin to suspect that here is a classic example of the gender and cultural imperialism that Rhys had to measure herself against. As Ford assumed the role of literary mentor he also assumed the role of lawgiver, his strategies here enacting the very processes of domination which Foucault analyses in 'The Order of Discourse' and which feminist and post-colonial theorists have invoked.[5] His Preface speaks for Rhys in ways which parallel imperialist discourse, where 'master codes of recognition' prescribe the perspective from which the 'other' may be seen.

Ford's Preface assumes a position of urbane authority as his 'I' strolls through the Left Bank in a narrative of personal reminiscence, laying out a topography which is both geographical and metaphorical. He prescribes the territory within which Rhys's stories may be read, that of modernist cosmopolitan Paris of the 1920s. He is more negligent about issues connected with women and colonialism, presenting Rhys as an exotic and emotional female with an 'instinct for form':

> Coming from the Antilles, with a terrifying insight and a terrific – an almost lurid! – passion for stating the case of the underdog, she has let her pen loose on the Left Banks of the Old World (*LB*, p.24).

He ends curiously with an adulatory elegy, placing Rhys somewhere where she would certainly not wish to be, imagining her ashes translated to the Pantheon in a 'voluminous pall' where he too hopes to figure: 'a grain or so of my scattered and forgotten dust may go in too, in the folds' (*LB*, p.27). That Ford's strategies of appropriation succeeded is clear from the fact that this collection is usually referred to as *The Left Bank*, and in the responses of contemporary reviewers who accepted Ford's perspective so unquestioningly that they could not see what Rhys's stories were doing. Instead, they concentrated on the Preface, praising it for its 'easy authority about the particular qualities of Parisian bohemianism' and contrasting this with 'Miss Rhys's sketches' which seem 'almost tentative'.[6] What readers failed to see was Rhys's distinctive achievement, for *The Left Bank* is her feminised version of *The Waste Land*, and her stories resist the territorialising imperative of Ford's Preface. To continue the metaphor, her stories occupy the spaces that Ford's narrative merely glances at or blanks out, as she writes about the 'others' whom Ford ignored in his wanderings. Interestingly, Ford complained in his Preface about her refusal to present a coherent geography of Montparnasse which would orient the reader: ' "Where did all this take place? What sort of places are these?" So I have butted in' (*LB*, p.26). Indeed Rhys's collection does present a figurative geography which is wider in its extension than Ford allows, but it is as fragmented as Eliot's *The Waste Land* and as hallucinatory on occasions as Djuna Barnes's *Nightwood*. Every story has its own microtopography: a room or a cafe – which may be in Paris, Vienna, Budapest or Dominica – a prison cell or a street; every story has its own strong sense of individual subjective positioning; and her refusals of Ford's prescriptions for coherence represent a deliberate policy of situating her stories outside his 'Rive Gauche' perameters while occupying secret places within the same territory.

Fourteen stories are set in Montparnasse, though that arrangement is dislocated by the intrusion of two stories set in the Santé prison and one in a hospital, plus two retrospective views of Dominica, while the last three effect a displacement from the Left Bank altogether. Two are set on the Riviera and the last one 'Vienne' sketches the deracinated European post-war world of 1921 in a series of anecdotes where the narrative moves restlessly from Vienna to Budapest to Prague, ending not with a return to Paris but with yet another prospect voiced in two languages, 'Nach London'. In a startling variety of narrative forms which include sketches, dramatic monologues and shapely stories with their moments of epiphany, Rhys has constructed her modernist short story collection on a principle of discontinuity which resists any master discourse. Rhys does not attempt to construct either a coherent map or an overriding metanarrative. The stories are told from the perspective of the 'others' (who are usually female though occasionally they are disadvantaged male colonials or foreigners), and they are all versions of the persistent Rhys theme, which Pearl Hochstadt calls 'the condition of alienation and vulnerability'.[7] Flashes of insight reveal secrets and private fantasy lives which are best kept hidden, in a world of surfaces where illusion not truth offers the most likely means of survival. Her Paris does not lack specificity, though her sketches of the cosmopolitan clientele of the Bal Musette on a Saturday night suggests an ironic distance from its ethos:

> For they are very intelligent, all these people. They paint, they write, they express themselves in innumerable ways. It is Chelsea, London, with a large dash of Greenwich Village, New York, and a slight sprinkling of Moscow, Christiana, and even of Paris to give incongruous local colourings. ('Tout Montparnasse and a Lady', *LB*, p.54)

For a feminist critic the main fascination lies in the women's stories. Rhys's Paris, for all its bohemianism, is a place which pays close attention to the codes of gender, class and money, and she is acutely aware of the determinisms this nexus imposes on women. These stories rehearse a variety of constructions of the feminine, together with examples of male indifference and cruelty; some tales of female revenge and mutual exploitation; more frequently stories of women's suicidal desperation and female romantic fantasies. Though we catch a glimpse of the faded woman who was to become the typical Rhys heroine in her later novels, she is kept at a distance here and we get close to her only once, in the Zanzi-Bar halfway up the Boulevard Montparnasse:

> Miss Dufreyne, for such was the Lady's name, was a weak, sentimental, very lazy, entirely harmless creature, pathetically incapable of lies or intrigue or even of self-defence – till it was too late. She was also sensual, curious, reckless, and had all her life roused a strong curiosity in men. So much for her. ('In the Rue de l'Arrivee,' *LB*, p.115)

The accent here is on youth, on the *petites femmes*, the dancers, the mannequins, and the *grues de Paris*, those sellers of illusion who make their precarious living by exploiting male fantasies of the feminine:

> Paris is sentimental and indulgent towards them. That, in the mass and theoretically of course, not always practically or to individuals. ('In a Cafe', *LB*, p.51)

The story of a *grue* is sketched in three verses of a cafe song:

> The first told the pathetic story of the making of a *grue;* the second told of her virtues, her charity, her warm-heartedness, her practical sympathy; the third, of the abominable ingratitude that was her requital. (*LB*, p.51)

The insignificance of such a girl's fate is made plain when, after the tumultuous applause, the song is displaced by one celebrating the face of American domesticity, 'Mommer loves Popper' paid for by an American girl in the audience. It is an ironic celebration of American incomprehension and the power of American money. But Rhys's stories of the *grues,* while acknowledging their common narrative, insist on separating the surface layer from the darker underside, offering instead a double vision of illusion and the secret lives of individual women hidden within. As Alicia Borinsky's essay, 'Jean Rhys: Poses of a Woman as Guest' suggests, the illusions of femininity are deliberate artifice more intimately related to questions of economics than to eroticism. Being more explicitly political than Rhys, Borinsky points to the relationship between 'the woman in Jean Rhys's texts and whoever gives the money. As the bills go from hand to hand, we perceive the desperation in the question about *what* to wear, for it stands for the fear of being alone, of not having not a *what* but a *whom* to wear. These women are victims of a pact that is never quite questioned: they dress and act for a male gaze that will, inevitably, humiliate them in the end.' [8] Rhys is fascinated by the dramatic enactment of the sexual and social economy in the European *demimonde* of the 1920s, which she sees as a patriarchal world where women are luxury items to be bought, enjoyed and discarded. The mannequins who emerge from the fashion houses in the evenings, making the streets as 'gay and as beautiful as beds of flowers before they walked swiftly away and the Paris night swallowed them up' (*LB*, p.70) have their counterparts in the Viennese *danseuses* who are briefly raved about and fêted, only to disappear without trace. Such women are marginal notes in male metanarratives of sexual and economic domination.

For Rhys, even women with private means were not exempt from the gendered narrative. The first story in the collection, 'Illusion', is about such a woman, the British expatriate painter Miss Bruce, who with her 'neat serge dress' and her 'neat tweed costume' would seem to assert her rights to independence. However, the story turns on the accidental revelation of Miss Bruces's secret locked away in her 'big, square, solid wardrobe': it is full of beautiful dresses, make-up jars, scents and fancy costumes, 'a collection of frocks' as she later has to admit. But it is more than an artist's collection, as the narrator intuits; these frocks encode the narrative of female fantasy and romance which has been studiously repressed; 'the perpetual hunger to be beautiful and that thirst to be loved which is the real curse of Eve' (*LB*, p.34). The story makes a statement about woman's condition: in a binary system of sexual power structures, a woman's appearance is always crucial. For Miss Bruce an image of independence is to be maintained only at the cost of becoming a mimic man.

The story of the woman artist forms an interesting contrast with that of Verhausen the Flemish painter in 'Tea with an Artist'. With the man the main focus is on his paintings but we never see any of Miss Bruce's, and her fantasies of the feminine look pathetically fragile beside Verhausen's painting of a woman:

> 'All the poisonous charm of the life beyond the pale was in her pose, in her smouldering eyes – all its deadly bitterness and fatigue in her fixed smile' (*LB*, p.78)

When the original appears in the person of Verhausen's ageing mistress, the narrator remarks on the difference between the 'heavy placid uninteresting woman' and the transformations effected by art. This might be read as Rhys's metafictional comment on the relation between her own art and its raw materials, but that reading would neglect the real woman's gesture at the end as she 'touched his cheek with her big hands . . . as it were the ghost of a time when her business in life had been the consoling of men' (*LB*, p.81). The coded message is about male/female difference; ironically it is the male artist who is protected and nurtured, while the female artist is alone, protecting her secret self as best she can behind locked doors and a male disguise.

Rhys's own position as a woman artist on the Left Bank has something in common with Miss Bruce's, though lacking her defences of Englishness and money. Like the locked wardrobe, this collection hides Rhys's secret life, which is her remembered childhood in Dominica, and three Caribbean stories hang in here, shimmering with 'a glow of colour, a riot of soft silks..a..everything that one did not expect' (*LB*, p.33). We hear the voices of others which are insinuated into the text of European modernism, for Rhys 'does not fit easily or completely within the context of modernist writing or women's fiction of her generation', as West Indian critic Veronica Gregg remarks.[9] In a manner rather like Miss Bruce's habit of staring over her listener's head as she defends her interest in frocks, Rhys introduces her Caribbean stories via a chance encounter in a Montparnasse restaurant with the coal black man in the smart grey lounge suit, the woman wearing Martinique costume and the Creole girl in the short red dress: 'It was because these were my compatriots that in that Montparnasse restaurant I remembered the Antilles' ('Trio,' *LB*, p.85). That first story focuses on the girl's gay defiance as she starts to sing and dance in the restaurant:

> Obviously the red dress was her only garment, obviously too she was exquisite beneath it . . . supple, slender, a dancer from the Thousand and One Nights . . .
> *J'en ai m-a-r-r-e.* (*LB*, p.84)

Already the girl's fate is encoded in her provocative self display, and the older woman's warning 'Keep yourself quiet, Doudou,' only emphasises the strong connection between the issues of gender and colonialism being made here, and the double disadvantage of being a colonial woman in a European culture.

Rhys turns away from Europe altogether in the next story 'Mixing Cocktails', a very personal narrative of a white West Indian woman remembering her childhood in Dominica. The story plunges into 'the house in the hills' with the telescope on the veranda through which 'you spied out the steamers passing' and the stars further away still. This is the place of dreams, where lying in the hammock the young girl spins her narrative about 'the endless blue day 'and her stories about being grown-up, being beautiful, being married, but those stories of the future are curiously uninhabited. Following a private emotional logic which is only thinly disguised by the pronoun shifts between 'I' and 'you' and 'one', the narrative sketches a distinctively colonial education in femininity with its clash of English and Caribbean voices: the aunt's exhortation to be 'like Other People', the old Obeah woman's advice , 'You all mustn't look too much at de moon', and the girl's moment of peace in the presence of her father 'working out his chess problem from The Times Weekly Edition' as she carries out her nightly duty of mixing cocktails: 'Here is something I can do.' (*LB*, p.92)

That private reminiscence of a colonial upbringing is balanced by a more public example of a classic colonial confrontation in 'Again the Antilles', as Rhys moves from gender to politics. The anecdote is about a heated correspondence in *The Dominica Herald and Leeward Islands Gazette* between its coloured editor Papa Dom and Mr Hugh Musgrave, 'an Englishman of the governing class'. It is not the cause of the feud which is important but the strategies adopted in this fierce exchange of letters, for the battle is about language and domination through discourse. As Helen Tiffin remarks, 'The dominant discourse enshrines the values of one particular culture as axiomatic, as literary or textual givens, and invokes policies of either assimilation or apartheid for the remainder of the English-speaking world'.[10] Papa Dom, a truly colonised subject, attempts to speak like the English, invoking Shakespeare in his rebuke to Mr Musgrave, but he makes the mistake of misattributing a quotation. Musgrave's reply is the predictable imperialist riposte:

> Dear Sir,
> I never read your abominable paper. But my attention has been called to a scurrilous letter about myself which you published last week. The lines quoted were written, not by Shakespeare but by Chaucer, though you cannot of course be expected to know that.' (*LB*, p.96).

After quoting the Chaucer impeccably, he ends with a remark about the names of great Englishmen 'being taken in vain by the ignorant of another race and colour'. The delight of the story is that Papa Dom refuses to be silenced and writes back again, invoking all the authority of the English tradition in his refutation of Mr Musgrave:

> I fail to see that it matters whether it is Shakespeare, Chaucer or the Marquis of Montrose who administers from down the ages the much-needed reminder and rebuke' (*LB*, p.97).

Rhys is carefully non-judgmental about the exchange, but for all its humour it highlights language as the site of the power struggle in a colonial culture.

As Rhys shows, imperialism has many voices, and the bland English tones of appropriation of another culture are heard at the beginning of 'La Grosse Fifi':

> 'The sea', said Mark Olsen, 'is exactly the colour of Rickett's blue this morning.'
> Roseau turned her head to consider the smooth Mediterranean. (*LB*, p.165) [11]

However, this story set in a cheap hotel on the Riviera shifts the accent to the power politics of gender in a woman's enslavement to romantic fantasy. Roseau, the young woman through whose consciousness the story is focalised, comes to know the secret story of the fat ageing Mme Francine Carly, commonly known as 'Fifi', whose passion for her gigolo ends in her being murdered by him.The title of Rhys's story recalls Maupassant's 'Mademoiselle Fifi' (1882) a tale about an episode in the Franco–Prussian War, but Rhys's narrative works in opposition to the main elements in Maupassant's.[12] His 'Fifi' figure is male, a thin and sadistic Prussian officer who is murdered – having his throat cut by a French Jewish tart when he shouts insults at the French people. It is an act of heroic revenge and Rachel the Jewess is rehabiliated by society as her reward. Rhys takes these plot elements and turns them around to tell her tale of female victimisation, of a woman who, caught in her romantic fantasy, willingly suffers the insults of her lover and is finally murdered in the same manner as her namesake in Maupassant. While the narrative interweaves two common versions of women's fate in their desperate search for love – Roseau's self pitying tale of a young woman 'searching for the godlike face of Love and finding always the grinning face of Lust' (*LB*, p.186) and Fifi's tale of unrequited love for a younger man – it is Fifi who is the focalised object here. Seen through the eyes of others, she is a grotesque old tart, a comforting friend and a mother figure, a sentimental fool and a reckless idealist. Her own perspective is presented only indirectly, when she voices her feelings by quoting French poetry. The poem is *Le Livre pour toi*, by Marguerite Burnat-Provins, and is a woman's song of joyous submission to her romantic ideal:[13]

> 'Chante, chante ma vie, aux mains de mon amant!'
>
> ....................
>
> And so on, and so on [as Roseau drily comments]
> Roseau thought that it was horrible to hear this ruin of a woman voicing all her own moods, all her own thoughts.
> Horrible. (*LB*, p.180)

What is celebrated in the poem is also celebrated in the story, as a different form of female heroism from Maupassant's: Fifi translates poetic fantasy into real life, and dies for it. The newspaper report of her murder with its generalisation, 'YET ANOTHER DRAMA OF JEALOUSY' is presented with the same clinical detachment as the reports of women's deaths in Joyce's 'A Painful Case' or Conrad's *The Secret Agent*. It carries a similar delayed charge of emotion, but in this particular painful case the moment of revelation is Fifi's parting gift to Roseau and the means of strengthening her to start anew:

> She imagined that she saw her friend's gay and childlike soul, freed from its gross body, mocking her gently for her sentimental tears . . .
>
> She dried her eyes and went on with her packing. (*LB*, p.191)

While such a story might cause the reader to contemplate the dangers of female fantasies of love and dependence, this response would seem beside the point here where the emphasis is on one woman's peculiar triumph in achieving her destiny.

Whereas 'La Grosse Fifi' is a tightly structured modernist

short story, 'Vienne', the last in the collection, is a fragmented narrative, dislocated in perspective, multivoiced and anecdotal as it ranges through the capitals of Europe. When the first version of 'Vienne' appeared in the *Transatlantic Review*, it consisted of three fragments, all sketches of women as male fantasy objects: 'The Dancer', 'Fischl', and 'The Spending Phase'. The *LB* version is much expanded into a wry *comédie humaine*:

> It seemed to be endless variations and inversions of a single chord – tuneless, plaintive melancholy; the wind over the plain, the hungry cry of the human heart and all the rest of it . . . Well, well . . . (*LB*, p.235)[14]

To the deracinated characters of Rhys's postwar *demi-monde* it is a matter of indifference whether the cafés, night clubs and hotels they drift through are in Vienna, Budapest, Paris or London. It is a febrile existence of desperate gaiety to be lived entirely in the present moment, where the female narrator adopts a shifting series of roles in response to circumstances over which she has no control. 'I was cracky with the joy of life that summer of 1921' (*LB*, p.202), yet by the end of the story she wishes to commit suicide. In such a precarious world, illusion is the only way of creating order out of the chaos of contingency.

Yet there is in this disrupted sequence a pattern of associations which determine its selection of anecdotes: they are all part of a kaleidoscopic narrative which figures the condition of being a woman in modern Europe. The feminine condition is variously illustrated through the anecdotes of the dancers, each of whom briefly represents 'sheer loveliness with a flame inside' (*LB*, p.194), only to be replaced by the pretty faces of other dancers, other mistresses:

> All the pretty people with doubtful husbands, or no husbands, or husbands in jail (lots of men went to jail – I don't wonder. Every day new laws about the exchange and smuggling gold). (*LB*, p.200)

On rare occasions a woman manages to win in the game of mutual exploitation, like 'Tillie the Avenger', another Tanzerin who cheats her lover out of 'every sou he possessed' (*LB*, p.208), but Tillie's triumph is balanced by the remarks on Viennese women passed by Colonel Mishima of the Interallied Disarmament Commission who refers to them collectively as 'war material' (*LB*, p.209) and by the arrogance of the 'Important Person' Fischl who promenades every evening 'choosing a woman'. Though the focalisation shifts to allow Mishima and Fischl to damn themselves in their own words, the narrator's role is fairly neutral until halfway through the story. Her own anxieties begin to surface, ironically enough, at the period when she and her husband have enough money for her to have a car and 'even the luxury of a soul' (*LB*, p.223). The new frankness penetrates the surface of Gelustige's story, the 'gr-r-r-ande cocotte' who knows the rules of the game:

> What a life that is; what courage it needs. The constant effort to please, the constant watch over one's nerves. Never to seem bored, never to seem at a loss.
> To learn to accept the most brutal rebuffs with a smile and keep one's dignity. (*LB*, p.227)

The narrator's own chagrin at the effort of keeping up appearances begins to show:

> Oh, abomination of desolation – to sit for two hours being massaged, to stand for hours choosing a dress. All to delight the eyes of the gentleman with the toothpick.
> (Who, finding me unresponsive has already turned his attention elsewhere.) (*LB*, p.229)

Such a lifestyle becomes increasingly difficult to maintain in the face of the threat of bankruptcy and charges of fraud which leave the narrator in a state of 'vague and bewildered fright' (*LB*, p.241) as her husband contemplates suicide. Instead of committing suicide, in this phantasmagoria of a world, 'of shadows, marionettes gesticulating on a badly lit stage' (*LB*, p.252), they flee in their large car, first to Budapest and then to Prague. The story ends with another unrealised suicide project, which is rather more the woman's wish than anything active, for she hoped that her husband would smash up the car and give 'the old hag Fate . . . the slip.' But such a climax would give a kind of inappropriate significance to a narrative whose only point is its pointlessness. Drunkenly the couple return to their hotel, facing the prospect of another displacement the next day, 'Nach London.'

There is no return to Paris as Rhys takes flight from Ford's prescribed territory, offering instead her own documentary of the modernist condition. She was an *étrangère* in the Kristevan sense long before Kristeva, whose critique, as Toril Moi says, 'undermines our most cherished convictions precisely because it situates itself outside our space, knowingly inserting itself along the borderlines of our own discourse.'[15] So much of Rhys's treatment of female difference, her analysis of representations of the feminine, and her subversive critiques of patriarchal metanarratives may be assimilated via postmodernist and feminist theory. But there is a difference, which may be one of period or which may be the difference between creative writing and theory: Jean Rhys does not write about 'La Femme' (this generalisation about women is what she deplores in her savage critiques of male discourse), but always about 'une femme' in all her jagged particularity, charting the contradictions, irresolutions, defeats and precarious survivals of individual women.

## *Quartet*

> When after a long struggle *Quartet* stopped being a record of facts and became a book a Book with a start a middle and an end where the characters sometimes talked and acted independently of me without my will I called it 'Masquerade' for already it had dawned on me the whole thing was pretending. Stella was pretending to be a sport I was pretending to be quite reckless . . . Ford was pretending, even Stephan [Lenglet] was pretending to suffer more than he really did . . . Anyway I changed to Quartet because I thought Masquerade had been used too much. So has Quartet. Then for some reason the publisher said that Quartet wouldn't do. I've always thought that I called it 'Postures' because I was sick of the whole thing and Postures was a meaningless title. But was it so meaningless? Hadn't it gone back to my first idea that it was all posturing all a pretence[16]

In Rhys's account in her Green Exercise Book, we have her double acknowledgement of personal experience and the transformations of art which actually reinvent life as fiction, at the same time acknowledging the unreality of real life itself. *Quartet* shifts the emphasis from masquerades and postures through its typically modernist figure of an image of order set in ironic contrast to a chaos of disordered emotions, but it also insists on a principle of interaction between four people within a closed structure dictated primarily by aesthetic convention. The 'facts' of the Rhys–Ford affair have been thoroughly researched by Martien Kappers-den Hollander, whose biographical essays themselves read like the outline for a modernist multivoiced novel about winning and losing in sexual games.[17] The facts as recorded by Kappers-den Hollander are these:

> While they were living in Paris in 1924, Lenglet was arrested by French authorities on the charge of petty embezzlement, and subsequently convicted. As he was serving his sentence in a prison outside Paris, Rhys was offered shelter in the home of her literary patron Ford Madox Ford and his common-law wife, the Australian painter Stella Bowen. The relationship developed into a *ménage à trois* that was to prove fatal to Rhys's marriage with Lenglet as well as to Ford's union with Bowen.[18]

Hollander's essays have all the fascination of gossip as she gives a detailed account of the other stories published after *Quartet*. Jean Lenglet published not one but three versions (in English, Dutch and French), telling the story from the betrayed husband's point of view in *Barred* (1932), *In de Strik* (1932) and *Sous les Verrous* (1933). Stella Bowen's version appears in her autobiography *Drawn from Life* (1941) where she attacks Rhys: 'I learnt what a powerful weapon lies in weakness and pathos and how strong is the position of the person who has nothing to lose'[19] Ford's novel *When the Wicked Man* (published 1931 and begun in Paris in December 1928 a few months after *Quartet* appeared) is his revenge for Rhys's portrait of him as Heidler; he replies by caricaturing Rhys in the figure of Lola Porter, 'a lewd and drunken Creole journalist'.[20] Curiously, one of his descriptions of Lola is savagely analagous to his praise of Rhys in the *Left Bank* Preface:

> She was a doomed soul, violent and demoralised . . . She took the lid off the world that she knew and showed us an underworld of darkness and disorder, where officialdom, the bourgeoisie, and the police were the eternal enemies.[21]

Rhys's interventions in Lenglet's versions are well known: it was she who translated *Sous les Verrous* into English and found it a publisher, in the process cutting between six-and-a-half and seven thousand words from his manuscript and revising the presentation of the main protagonists – most crucially of herself and of the Lenglet figure.[22] She also comments in the Green Exercise Book on Bowen's version much later, at the time of her furious reaction to the 'lies' in Arthur Mizener's biography of Ford, *The Saddest Story,* which she read in 1972: 'It did seem to me though that she'd left out suppressed so much that her version of things was completely false.' It is not known whether Rhys or Bowen or Lenglet ever read *When the Wicked Man*; nor do we know exactly when Rhys read *The Good Soldier,* though she would seem not to have read it till 1968: 'Ford's book [*The Good Soldier*] puzzles me a bit. I must read it again slowly and be convinced that it's the saddest story.[23]

Against and indeed prior to these other stories, Rhys offers a different version, one which is very close to female Gothic, though it is also true that the quartet figure makes it possible to take a distance from romantic fantasy, allowing connections to be made between male and female predicaments which the protagonists have failed to see. *Quartet* is riddled with transgressions, betrayals and entrapments, but as the text shows, this is not exclusive to Marya. Rhys's novel attempts to bind together the 'other stories' of victimisation and loss, though slanting the narrative towards a version that was not 'too unfair' to herself.[24] It is as if in Rhys's novel two versions of her affair with Ford overlap: the design indicates an awareness of Marya's limits of vision, but the narrative really belongs to her.[25] Marginal as Marya is shown to be in the stories of the other three protagonists, she is the central figure in her own, and her perspective displaces the others to the margins of her story. Though she is not there at the end of the novel, her husband's driving away with another woman is a fitting end to Marya's story of desertion and betrayal.

*Quartet* was seen as a modernist work by at least one contemporary reviewer, who compared it with Hemingway's *The Sun Also Rises* as a product of Gertrude Stein's Lost Generation.[26] Modernist, yes, in its setting, in its evocation of the glamorous world of postwar futility; but a modernist version of

Gothic. Indeed the novel is most interesting and disturbing to a feminist reader in its presentation of a female victim fantasy, as it develops in detail one possible construction of the feminine. Again Paris is the shifting cosmopolitan world of the Left Bank, but here it becomes a Gothic labyrinth, where cafés and studio parties take on the metaphorical dimensions of torture chambers and where prisons are real. It is Marya's sensibility that gives the narrative its Gothic colouration, for it is in her consciousness only that Paris is metamorphosed. As readers we are forced into complicity with Marya's point of view, hearing snatches of the others' stories which can only be accommodated in relation to their effects on her.

Marya is a young Englishwoman cast adrift in Paris when her husband is arrested and imprisoned for theft. Arguably she was adrift before that, a 'vagabond by nature'[27] married to a Polish emigré, a *'commissionaire d'objets d'art'* who had married her because she was another beautiful object, and they live a precariously marginal existence in a series of Paris hotels. She is the opposite of the liberated Anglo-Saxon woman in Paris of the twenties, though the novel presents three women painters who fill that role: Miss Da Solla, Lois Heidler and her American friend, Miss Nicholson. But Marya, separated from these women by crucial gaps of money and class, is as much an object to them as she is to men, 'a decorative little person' (*Q*, p.7 ) to be painted wearing green gloves and a black dress but not someone whose point of view on anything might be considered significant. Rhys's heroine is an anachronism in Paris with her unquestioning assumption of traditional gender roles and her commitment to the most dangerous of female romantic fantasies. Her story, criticised by the *New York Herald Tribune* reviewer as 'banal', offers a classic version of the fate of the innocent helpless victim caught up in the duplicities of social and sexual games that she does not understand.

Her relationship to the real world is always oblique: she exists in a curious borderland of sensation and emotion which is registered appropriately, not in the first person but in the third, through Marya's indirect interior monologue:

> It was astonishing how significant, coherent and understandable it all became after a glass of wine on an empty stomach . . . The Place

> Blanche, Paris. Life itself. One realized all sorts of things. The value of an illusion, for instance, and that the shadow can be more important than the substance . . . (*Q*, p.22–3)

Events never quite impinge on her, and her response to Stephan's arrest is the classic Gothic heroine's urge to flight:

> She spent the foggy day in endless, aimless walking, for it seemed to her that if she moved quickly enough she would escape the fear that hunted her. It was a vague and shadowy fear of something cruel and stupid that had caught her and would never let her go. (*Q*, p.33)

Marya offers herself as a victim in her fantasy of dread, presenting an image of helpless destitution in order to claim rescue and protection. From the beginning of her relationship with the Heidlers she is in the position of a dependent, firmly spelled out to her by Lois Heidler:

> When you told me that your husband was in jail – d'you remember? – I felt as if you'd stretched out a hand for help. Well – I caught hold of your hand. I want to help you. I'll be awfully disappointed and hurt if you don't allow me to. (*Q*, p.53)

She is once again an object – first of the Heidlers' charity, and then successively of Heidler's infatuation, of Lois's jealousy and hatred, and finally of the combined contempt of the Heidlers and of her husband. At the end Marya becomes an inanimate object left on the floor, 'crumpled up' and 'still'. The one position Marya seldom occupies is that of a subject, in the sense of being a self, constituted in and through language. The image she offers to the world is that of a blank space, allowing herself to be constructed through other people's narratives. She can best be characterised by her lack of character: there is nothing 'essential' about Marya. Just as she has 'no solidity and fixed background', so she lacks what Judith Kegan Gardiner calls 'a core configuration of self,'[28] existing as a discontinuous series of surface images in response to the demands of others. Her aspiration towards a condition of total dependence constitutes the kind of feminine appeal to male power fantasies which Stella Bowen so severely criticised in Rhys herself. Needing male authority to give her definition, she shifts from being

Stephan's 'petted, cherished child, the desired mistress, the worshipped perfumed goddess' (*Q*, p.22) to being Heidler's 'pretty thing'. Such fantasy images of course always define 'feminine' as 'other', either more or less than human, leaving no space to accommodate a living woman.[29] Marya prefers to exist in an alternative dreamlike world where male and female fantasies collude and collide in a complex system of mutual exploitation. She elevates men into gods (a point she herself wittily exposes in their visit to the church: 'God's quite a pal of yours?' 'Yes,' said Heidler. *Q*, p.96), granting them absolute power over her in a doublefaced narrative where her desire for protection creates the conditions for her own victimisation.

Though the story of Marya's affair with Heidler follows the configurations of Gothic victim fantasy and of Rhys's adolescent Mr Howard narrative (and to that extent plays out a gendered narrative intimately related to sex, desire and power), what is actually dramatised in this novel is spikier and more complex than the blueprint suggests. Marya's final silent prostration is a state to which she is reduced in the course of the narrative, not the point from which she began. Disadvantaged as she is by sex, class and lack of money, she does try to speak her resistance to the Heidlers' offer of shelter. She tries to assert her point of view in arguments with Lois about her marriage to Stephan, but having no language to counter Lois's middle-class certainties, she retreats into silence as a mask for dissent. Actually the unspoken subtext of her anger is so coherent that as readers we have difficulty in remembering that this is interior monologue and that Marya's surface is a blank. What she says in reply to one of Lois's questions is brief: 'I can't. I don't think about things in that way.' (*Q*, p.64) And then, 'She muttered: You don't understand.' (*Q*, p.52) What intervenes is a far more savage criticism of Lois:

> Words that she longed to shout, to scream, crowded into her mind: 'You talk and you talk and you don't understand. Not anything. It's all false, all second-hand. You say what you've read and what other people tell you. You think you're very brave and sensible, but one flick of pain to yourself and you'd crumple up.' (*Q*, p.64)

But all this, as so often with Rhys's heroines, is unsaid, for they do not assume a position of authority from which their voices can be heard.

Marya allows herself to be silenced by Lois, though always retaining a certain freedom to think and feel independently, even to the extent of feeling sorry for her. With Heidler however, her resistance is compromised from the start, caught as she is in her own romantic fantasy. Indeed even Marya's perception of Heidler's brutality and her initial rage at his proposals serve to confirm her prescribed role as sexual victim. Any resistance she offers is met by Heidler with categorical statements of denial: 'Rubbish!' said Heidler tenderly. 'Rubbish.' And a bit later, 'In spite of you I'll do it.' (*Q*, p.77) This is the discourse of male dominance to which Marya seems programmed to succumb – and she almost willingly (or rather willessly) enters into a kind of complicity with Heidler's fantasy because it has its exact feminine counterpart in her own:

> When he took her in his arms she thought: 'How gentle he is. I was lost before I knew him. All my life before I knew him was like being lost on a cold, dark night.' She shivered. Then she smiled and shut her eyes again. (*Q*, p.83)

This condition of living with one's eyes shut to the real world of action and consequences is the one Marya ardently yearns to occupy. It is the perilous territory of female romantic fantasy which exists outside the social order, where being in love means being possessed physically and spiritually; of existing in a state beyond volition and identity. Rhys never tries to explain male domination. She proceeds more subtly by exploring the condition of feminine lack through a particularly disturbing scenario of desire where enclosed spaces of refuge become prisons and places of torment, and where woman's inescapable condition is that of total prostration to the man who is both lover and torturer. As erotic fantasy its Gothic features seem to collude with the fantasy images of much male pornography.[30]

It is characteristic of Rhys's double vision that she should present Marya's fantasy within the context of real life, and that Marya herself should have flashes of insight into her predicament. One such flash occurs as she sits, eyes open this time, facing the Heidlers in a railway carriage:

> It seemed to her that, staring at the couple, she had hypnotised herself into thinking, as they did, that her mind was part of their minds and that she understood why they so often said in exactly the same tone of puzzled bewilderment: 'I don't see what you're making such a fuss about' . . . There they were. And there Marya was: haggard, tormented by jealousy, burnt up by longing.' (*Q*, p.98)

But her reasonable assessment of her position as the 'other woman' is powerless against the spell of Heidler's authority and the 'unutterable sweet peace' of surrender to him.

Gradually Marya gives up, allowing herself to be installed in a seedy hotel overlooking Montparnasse station, where she spends a great deal of time stretched out on the huge bed looking at the wallpaper and waiting for Heidler to visit her. Trapped in her obsession yet always aware of the conditions of her entrapment, Marya is simultaneously conscious of Heidler's contempt for her, even as she succumbs to his physical strength and his fantasies. It is an odd position of insight and blindness that she occupies:

> But he did it with such conviction that she, miserable weakling that she was, found herself trying to live up to his idea of her.
> She lived up to it. And she had her reward.
> ' . . . You pretty thing – you pretty, pretty thing. Oh, you darling . . .
> Are you all right for money? I'd better leave some money, hadn't I? (*Q*, pp 118–9)

Against Marya's narrative, Heidler invokes the discourse of the social order with its prescriptive codes of recognition and prohibition that blank out the discourse of desire, including his own, which can be recuperated as an affair with a prostitute. Increasingly, as he tires of her, Heidler insists on the 'rules of the game', a strategy which Marya recognises as the language of imperialism. There are provocative though unstated connections between Heidler's calling her a 'savage' in his love talk and Marya's comparison between him and Queen Victoria, connections underlined when she is forced to 'play the game' by attending one of Lois's parties, 'feeling like a captive attached to somebody's chariot wheels' (*Q*, p.115).

Despite Marya's silencing, Rhys constructs for her an internal discourse which runs as subtext to the main narrative.

Indeed this is her only novel where Rhys directly addresses female sexuality, using what Ford would call 'lurid' images of pain:

> If this was love – this perpetual aching longing, this wound that bled persistently and very slowly. And the devouring hope. And the fear. That was the worst. The fear she lived with – that the little she had would be taken from her.
> Love was a terrible thing. You poisoned it and stabbed at it and knocked it down into the mud – well down – and it got up and staggered on, bleeding and muddy and awful. Like – like Rasputin. Marya began to laugh. (*Q*, p.122–3)[31]

There is an enormous gap between this fractured internal monologue with its vividly pulsating images and surface effects, where Marya appears as one of the living dead:

> Her eyelids were swollen and flaccid over unnaturally large bright eyes. Her head seemed to have sunk between her shoulders, giving her a tormented and deformed look. Her mouth drooped, her skin was greyish, and when she made up her face the powder and rouge stood out in clownish patches. (*Q*, p.124)

Marya's consciousness, if such a state can be so called, has become the site of conflicting discourses of desire for Heidler, of nostalgia for her former life with Stephan, and of jealous hatred for Lois:

> A dream. A dream. '*La vie toute faite des morceaux. Sans suite comme des rêves*'. Who wrote that? Gaugin. '*Sans suite comme des rêves.*' A dream. Long shining empty streets and tall dark houses looking down at her. (*Q*, p.123)

To Heidler such agony is impermissible excess which must be banished, for 'he was thinking it wouldn't do to leave the girl trailing round Montparnasse looking as ill as all that' (*Q*, p.153). Refusing to listen to Marya, Heidler sends her off to Cannes 'to forget everything and get well'. But Marya insists on writing her pain:

> It's as if all the blood in my body is being drained, very slowly, all the time, all the blood in my heart. What can I say to make you believe me? (*Q*, p.156)

The answer, as Marya finds, is nothing. Heidler in reply sends an envoy to silence her on the pretext that 'Lois thought you must be seedy' (*Q*, p.159). Like the fox that she and the envoy Miss Nicholson see in the zoological gardens, Marya too will be contained; neither her pain nor the fox's is allowed to signify within the codes of civilised social discourse:

> It would strike its nose, turn and run again. Up and down, up and down, ceaselessly. A horrible sight, really. 'Sweet thing,' said Miss Nicholson., (*Q*, p.160)

Expelled from her dream world, Marya becomes an exile in real life as represented by the social contract of her marriage. On Stephan's return from prison she finds she has no place in his urgent narrative of flight, and she makes a last painful attempt to re-enter the locked room of her fantasy. Standing against the door of their hotel bedroom, she shouts at Stephan her passion for Heidler: 'I love him.' A delicious relief flooded her as she said the words and she screamed again louder: 'I love him! I love him!' (*Q*, p.184) In what is a very theatrically constructed scene, the open door represents no exit for her, as Stephan takes his revenge for what he sees as betrayal, knocking her down and leaving her 'crumpled up' on the floor. '*Voilà pour toi*,' said Stephan. (*Q*, p.186)

The end of the novel shifts abruptly to Stephan's exit, in a shabby replay of the sexual game from his point of view. The Heidler narrative vanishes with Marya's loss of consciousness, and in its place is a short brutal scenario representing the duplicities in male fantasies about women. Women here are not even objects of desire, but objects of contempt or *objets trouvés*, women as temptresses, women as mothers:

> At that moment women seemed to him loathsome, horrible – soft and disgusting weights suspended round the necks of men, dragging them downwards. At the same time he longed to lay his head on Mademoiselle Chardin's shoulder and weep his life away.
> She put her warm hand over his firmly and said:
> 'My little Stephan, don't worry.'
> The taxi rattled on towards the Gare de Lyon. (*Q*, p.186)

Stephan himself comes to represent a distorted reflection of

Marya's helpless condition, which of course she is not there to see.

In her first full-length representation of the feminine, Rhys tells the story of the female victim left damaged, unconscious or dead, by the men whom she had successively invested with power over her: it is this version of romantic fantasy gone sour that Rhys was to tell over and over again. Neither Marya nor Lois Heidler nor Mademoiselle Chardin challenges the male metanarrative in *Quartet*. Instead they are all shown to be collaborators in a collective fantasy about male power and female submission. It is the paradox of Rhys's version of femininity that, though she offers a merciless exposure of women's vulnerability, her stories make no attempt to unsettle the traditional balance of power between the sexes. Rather, women's fantasies continue to sustain it.

# Chapter Three

# *'It Might Have Been Anywhere'*: After Leaving Mr Mackenzie

Whereas *Quartet* constructs its version of the feminine through a Gothic female victim fantasy of being locked into a romantic obsession, *After Leaving Mr Mackenzie* is a novel about a woman being locked out from what she desires most. As its title suggests, separation is the main thematic motif – separation from others and a more terrifying separation within the subject herself. This, the most forlorn of all Rhys's novels, is an anxious investigation of the modernist condition of exile, from a feminine perspective: how this might be experienced by a woman cast adrift in Paris and London; and the consequences of this exiled condition for a woman's narrative. In this context of anxieties of representation, I would like to take up Deborah Kelly Kloepfer's remark about the way in which representation becomes 'both "baffled" – balked or deflected ["distorted" is Rhys's word] – and "baffling" – perplexing , bewildering' – in this novel.[1] Arguably this bafflement experienced by the female protagonist and by other characters in the novel might also be read as Rhys's own self reflexive comment on writing fiction. Julia Martin's sceptical questions about why a woman bothers to try to tell her story when nobody wants to hear it are also

Rhys's questions about writing that story. These doubts might be seen to be amply confirmed by the contemporary *Times Literary Supplement* reviewer's remark that it was all 'a waste of talent'[2]. This is a catalogue of failed relationships which finds its focus in Julia's central failure to wrest any significance from the narrative of her life. I would suggest that her failed quest for meaning is paralleled in the structure of the novel itself, where its doublings and shifting perspectives generate an interplay of signifiers which, in their incompleteness, tease and baffle the reader much as Julia herself is baffled by the unframed oil painting of 'a half empty bottle of wine, a knife and a piece of Gruyère cheese' standing on the ledge of her room in the Hotel St Raphael, where 'every object in the picture was slightly distorted and full of obscure meaning.'[3]

The question asked insistently is the same question Virginia Woolf asks in *To the Lighthouse* when faced with the disorder and arbitrariness of life: 'What does it mean then? What can it all mean?'[4] Woolf's fiction gives at least a partial answer in her 'moments of being' when life seems to resolve itself temporarily into stability and order. David Lodge in *Modes of Modern Writing* finely distinguishes Woolf's feminine moments of transcendence from the masculine epiphanies of Joyce, Yeats's 'unity of being', and Eliot's 'still points redeemed from time'. While arguing that such privileged moments of aesthetic and spiritual revelation are one of the characteristic features of modernist writing, Lodge goes on to describe Woolf's peculiarly deconstructive approach: 'In short, Virginia Woolf's modernist insistence on the relativity and subjectivity of experience undermines the redeeming power of the privileged moment, because the moment is never shared'[5]. Rhys too adopts Woolf's 'alien and critical' perspective, but her protagonists' exiled condition leaves them a stage further back even from Woolf's provisional answer. Despite their yearning, the moment of revelation never comes; epiphany hovers for Julia Martin but meaning dissolves before it can be apprehended, leaving her outside the mystery, with only an irretrievable sense of loss.

The *T.L.S.* reviewer (5 March, 1931) summarised *After Leaving Mr Mackenzie* with a marked lack of sympathy for its subject:

> This book is an episode in the life of a prostitute. Julia Martin

> followed her inclinations with comparative ease and pleasure until Mr Mackenzie had finished with her. It is difficult to see why leaving so unattractive a person as Mr Mackenzie should have broken Julia's spirit. Least of all did Julia herself understand it, living as she did, entirely without plan, led by her emotions and resigned to her fate. After the break she goes from man to man. They are sorry for her, but they no longer want her. They give her a pound to two to go away; she takes it and goes. The sordid little story is written with admirable clarity and economy of language. But it leaves one dissatisfied. It is a waste of talent.

Though this review highlights one of the important separations that occurs at this period in Julia's life, it neglects another that is far more crucial: her mother's death. Emphasis on the heterosexual narrative leads to over-simplification not only of Julia's responses ('Least of all did Julia herself understand it') but also of the novel's structure, which is a record of multiple separations and failed relationships recounted from different characters' perspectives and enacted and re-enacted several times in the novel. Julia has already left Mr Mackenzie six months before this story opens, but the novel begins and ends with two more meetings and partings between them in a situation of potentially infinite repetition. Her mother's death brings back memories of earlier separations stretching back to childhood, just as Julia's rejection by her sister and her uncle is replayed several times, with variations, between her arrival in London and her final departure after the funeral. With its doubling back into memory and its incessant replay of crisis scenes, this is the opposite of a simple linear narrative, reconstructing instead a damaged female psyche for whom the present is inseparable from the past. Far from being just a 'sordid little story' about an ageing prostitute, Julia's is a narrative about a failed mother–daughter relationship as much as it is about failed relationships between men and women. In both cases the feminine principle is discredited by society and denied any significance. Julia's loss is articulated through a whole series of separations, so that she ends up alone and adrift, sitting in a Paris boulevard café over a drink which has been paid for by a man who has already left her, in a state of total apathy and an exile from her family and her country.

The novel opens with a flat narrative statement: 'After she had parted from Mr Mackenzie, Julia Martin went to live in a cheap hotel on the Quai des Grands Augustins.' (*ALMM*, p.9) Then the narrative gradually shifts to internal focalisation through Julia's consciousness (though always preserving the indeterminacy of the indirect interior monologue), registering her emotional damage as a result of the failed affair:

> And she had told herself that it was a good sort of place to hide in. She had also told herself that she would stay there until the sore and cringing feeling, which was the legacy of Mr Mackenzie, had departed. (*ALMM*, p.11)

His 'legacy' includes a weekly maintenance cheque, sent by his lawyer. Sexual power politics are vividly illustrated here with Mr Mackenzie's male discourse of dominance exerting his authority even in his absence through the language of money and the law. Julia's response is a combination of hatred and anger which must be imprisoned/unspoken in order for her to survive at all in her dependent condition, for 'It seemed to her that there were no limits at all to their joint powers of defeating and hurting her.' (*ALMM*, p.22)

This polarisation is established before the novel's *point de départ*, which is the day on which Mackenzie's last cheque arrives. Threatened with destitution, Julia's first emotion is rage at Mr Mackenzie combined with a sense of her 'dreary and abject humiliation.' The reasons for her rage are more fully explained in the draft version, for in characteristic manner Rhys deleted heavily in her revisions:

> She remembered every detail of then and she remembered that he had despised and insulted her . . . Now she was dismissed with a little present as small as he could [End of fragment]. As she walked along the six months of resignation were blotted out and she knew that she must find Mr Mackenzie and have things out with him and find out why he had behaved as he did. She must do this or go mad.[6]

Aware of her own powerlessness but desperate for revenge, Julia tracks down Mr Mackenzie and confronts him in the Restaurant Albert. This is an astonishing scene, focused successively through two male points of view, though never through Julia's. Seen from Mr Mackenzie's perspective, Julia rises up like an unwelcome ghost from the past, conjured by his own thoughts about her:

> Mr Mackenzie began to think about Julia Martin. He did this as seldom as possible, but the last time he had seen her had been in that restaurant. Now he remembered her unwillingly. (*ALMM*, pp.24–5)

While thinking that he had not been 'ungenerous', he lifted his eyes '– and there she was, coming in at the door' (*ALMM*, p.28). In the confrontation which follows, we hear very little of their conversation; Julia talks 'volubly' but she has no voice that Mr Mackenzie will listen to. 'She said' is repeated at intervals seven times, but her words blur through Mr Mackenzie's focalisation as he insists to himself on the banality of this situation:

> Surely even she must see that she was trying to make a tragedy out of a situation that was fundamentally comical. The discarded mistress – the faithful lawyer defending the honour of the client . . . A situation consecrated as comical by ten thousand farces and a thousand comedies. (*ALMM*, p.30-1)

Mr Mackenzie's only change of feeling is to one of embarrassment when Julia raises her voice in accusation, but when she strikes him on the face with her glove he does not even blink. Julia's challenge only stimulates him to stare her down, which he does, till Julia acknowledges that she is beaten, when, 'to Mr Mackenzie's unutterable relief, she gathered up her gloves and walked out of the restaurant.' (*ALMM*, p.26)

This is another instance of the male gaze, used here not to objectify women as erotic objects but to overpower them (as Mr Rochester will do later in a similar manner to Antoinette). Mr Mackenzie stares at Julia from his position of respectability within the social order from which she is excluded. That same exclusion was coded earlier in the scene through the unspoken male language of eyes too, for when Julia appeared in the restaurant, M.Albert the proprietor had glanced 'significantly' at Mackenzie as if to ask, 'Do you want to have her put out?' and Mackenzie had 'tried to telegraph back, "Not yet, anyhow. But stand by" ' (*ALMM*, p.29). All this happened before he even looked directly at Julia standing opposite him.

There is another male gazer in the restaurant too, and the scene is replayed from an angle behind Mr Mackenzie's head through the eyes of Mr George Horsfield. He had seen it all reflected in the mirror, 'A bad looking glass too. So that the actors had been slightly distorted, as in an unstill pool of water' (*ALMM*, p.37). His attitude of detached sympathy leads him to go in search of Julia, but the view point is still male; there is nothing from Julia's point of view at all, for she is not a signifying subject when the male point of view governs the narrative. This dual focalisation presents a rather hostile construction of masculine subjectivity, not unlike that in *To the Lighthouse* which has been analysed by Rachel Bowlby and by Pierre Bourdieu, both of whom characterise the masculine as rational, linear, and socially conditioned to roles of domination against which women are positioned as 'other' in a polarised pattern of gender roles.[7]

Unlike some of Rhys's heroines, Julia is not silent; indeed she makes repeated attempts to tell the story of her life: to Mr Mackenzie, to George Horsfield, earlier to a woman sculptor for whom she sat as a model, to Mr James her first lover whom she goes to see in London. But nobody is willing to listen, and if they are forced to hear they disbelieve and distrust her. She cannot find an appropriate language through which to represent herself and her experiences, so that her story is forced into the subtext of the narrative. Julia remains opaque to the men in her life; they do not want to know her, preferring to reconstruct an image of her in terms of their fantasies of the feminine. As Julia tells Horsfield, 'I was for sleeping with – not for talking to.' (*ALMM*, p.173). She may be a speaking subject, but she is not a signifying subject, and it is this lack of significance that defeats her. In trying to tell her past life, words turn against her, rendering her inauthentic even to herself, so that her telling becomes the opposite of a conventional affirmation of identity.[8] Instead she realises that her narrative is only a series of constructions like any other, where connections between past and present are merely the effect of artifice, giving the lie to any concept of an essential self. Her past self – or selves, for there are so many different stories – stand(s) always at a distance from the present, so that Julia splits to become a ghost, haunting her own life. This odd perception occurs several times: after telling her story to the woman sculptor, and on her return to London when in Tottenham Court Road she sees her younger self coming out of the fog to meet her:

> The ghost was thin and eager . . . It drifted up to her and passed her in the fog. And she had the feeling that, like the old man, it looked at her coldly, without recognizing her.(*ALMM*, p.68)

Memory is transformed via the metaphor of the *doppelganger*, which then colludes with the rest of society against Julia in a powerful image not only of isolation but of self-estrangement.

It might be argued that Julia's repeated separations from Mr Mackenzie are only symptoms of her malaise, distorted reflections of the central separation of her life, that of separation from her mother.[9] Certainly it would be characteristic of Rhys's riddling strategies in this novel and of its insistent pattern of doubles and surrogates, and certainly it is Julia's mother's death which 'breaks her up' rather then her separation from Mr Mackenzie. Returning to London apparently on a whim, Julia discovers that her mother is dying and so she stays until after the death and the funeral, before going back to Paris utterly bereft of hope and emptied out of feeling. When Julia sees her, the dying woman is speechless and paralysed, 'a huge shapeless mass under the sheets and blankets' (*ALMM*, p.97), an image interpreted by Kloepfer in her study of absent mothers as 'a trope for textlessness'. However, the scenes when Julia is with her mother (which are also those parts of the novel when focalisation through her consciousness is most sustained and intense) do not centre on the mother's muteness but on Julia's desire for all that 'mothering' represents: care, approval, her lost childhood, and that impossible state of wholeness when her mother had been 'the warm centre of the world.' What Julia urgently needs is a sign of unconditional maternal recognition, and some of the affection which she craves is expressed in her childlike greeting to her mother as she says in a 'frightened, hopeful voice: "I'm Julia, do you know? It's Julia." ' (*ALMM*, p.98) But that is not what she gets, for the only sign of recognition is a glare which she takes as the sign of total disapproval. Julia and her sister Norah stand at the foot of their mother's bed giggling hysterically at a bad joke, in a parodic version of the dying parent scene:

> Then she saw her mother's black eyes open again and stare back into hers with recognition and surprise and anger. They said, 'Is this why you have come back? Have you come back to laugh at me?' Julia's heart gave a horrible leap into her throat.
> She said, 'Norah, she does know me. I'm sure she does'. (*ALMM*, p.100)

As Julia interprets it, her mother has done what she dreaded most, for she too has 'put her outside the pale, as everybody else had done' (*ALMM*, p.96), and her sister underlines that sense of exclusion by sending Julia out of her mother's room because her mother seems to be upset by the presence of 'anybody strange'.

Yet Julia's desire is so intense that she can conjure the lost dream of childhood back when sitting beside her mother's inert figure, 'remembering it so vividly that mysteriously it was all there again' (*ALMM*, p.107). Here the manuscript version is even more explicit about the maternal principle:

> And sitting there near her you felt peaceful. You felt that there you'd find an answer to the questions that tormented you.[10]

Julia catches up with her mother only at the moment of her vanishing, and the moment of death re-enacts yet again that crucial separation, without any revelation or relief: ' "Gone." That was the word.' (*ALMM*, p.123)

It is at the funeral service that Julia makes her last effort to grapple for significance against her mother's absence, but again she is baffled by a confusion of signifiers:

> She was obsessed with the feeling that she was so close to seeing the thing that was behind all this talking and posturing, and that the talking and the posturing were there to prevent her from seeing it. Now it's time to get up; now it's time to kneel down; now it's time to stand up.
>
> But all the time she stood, knelt, and listened she was tortured because her brain was making a huge effort to grapple with nothingness. And the effort hurt; yet it was almost successful. In another minute she would know. And then a dam inside her head burst, and she leant her head on her arms and sobbed. (*ALMM*, p.130)

Yet through her tears, Julia is vouchsafed a characteristically dual moment of revelation, an ambiguous and undecodable epiphany which suggests strong psychic links between the daughter and the maternal principle at the very time of the destruction of her mother's body:

> She was crying now because she remembered that her life had been a long succession of humiliations and mistakes and pains and ridiculous efforts. Everybody's life was like that. At the same time, in a miraculous manner, some essence of her was shooting upwards like a flame. She was great. She was a defiant flame shooting upwards not to plead but to threaten. Then the flame sank down again, useless, having reached nothing. (*ALMM*, p.131)

The imagery is apocalyptic but its resonances are intensely subjective, and for Julia they seem to betoken destruction rather than transformation. She is, however, sufficiently energised by this brief insight to strike out not once but twice at middle-class respectability and its bankrupt morality, embodied for her in her sister Norah and her Uncle Griffiths, accusing Norah of being 'eaten up with jealousy' and her uncle of being 'an abominable old man' (*ALMM*, p.136). So she wrests for herself a moment of peace, alone in her mother's empty bedroom, before being shut out of the family home forever.

The narrative plays off Julia's intensely focused relation with her mother against the ironic counterpoint of her affair with George Horsfield. Utterly bereft after her mother's funeral, she spends that same evening with Horsfield and invites him up to her hotel room where she goes to bed with him, simply to avoid being on her own. This is the chapter which the narrator entitles 'It Might Have Been Anywhere', suggesting both the banality of this encounter and Julia's anaesthesia. The sexual act itself is hidden within the blurred focus of the participants' responses and is more a forlorn image of separation than of union:

> You are thirsty, dried up with thirst, and yet you don't know it until somebody holds up water to your mouth and says: 'You're thirsty, drink.' It's like that. You are thirsty, and you drink.
>
> And then you wonder all sorts of things, discontentedly and disconnectedly.

> 'But the worst of it is,' he thought, 'That one can never know what the woman is really feeling.' (*ALMM*, p.153)

While Horsfield, who is not without sensitivity, perceives the 'child' in Julia, he has no inkling of the dimensions of her loss nor can he know 'what the woman is really feeling.' Her deepest wish against all logic, is for contact with her mother. Curiously this is granted to her, but in a terrifyingly Gothic encounter where the sexual relationship again functions as a form of displacement and where Horsfield is cast by Julia not in the role of lover but of mother-surrogate. It is when they are returning to Julia's room the next night that the bizarre incident on the staircase occurs. It takes place entirely in darkness, when Horsfield, having passed Julia on the stairs, reaches out and gently runs his fingers over her hand and her arm and then touches the fur collar of her coat. But his erotic enjoyment is interrupted by Julia's panic-stricken cry:

> She said in a loud voice: 'Oh God, who touched me?'
> He was too much astonished to answer.
> 'Who touched me?' she screamed. 'Who's that? Who touched my hand? What's that?'
> 'Julia!' he said.
> But she went on screaming loudly: 'Who's that? Who's that? Who touched my hand?'
> 'Well,' thought Mr Horsfield, 'That's torn it.' (*ALMM*, p.163)

Not only is this a reminder that the man and the woman are each locked away from the other in totally separate subjective dimensions, but the reader too is as shocked as Horsfield by Julia's screaming. Her explanation when it comes, explains nothing to him:

> 'I thought it was – someone dead,' she muttered, 'catching hold of my hand.'
> 'Oh, Julia, my dear, look here, you're sick. Let me help you.' (*ALMM*, p.165)

If Julia is sick, she is also beyond any help that Horsfield can give her at this moment when her deepest desire has been projected as hallucinatory contact with the dead. There is no means by which Horsfield can communicate with her, and finally he has to realise that she is totally indifferent to him.

Julia's separation from Horsfield and her departure from London is told from his perspective, as the reader watches him retreating from a position of sympathy for the woman to a more distanced and 'theoretical' state of mind which is far less threatening of his own sense of self security. Without knowing it, he comes to occupy a similar position to Julia's other lovers, and like Mr Mackenzie and Mr James he views her departure with relief. His return to his own house is recorded with Rhys's characteristic elision between internal and external narrative focalisation:

> He shut the door and sighed. It was as if he had altogether shut out the thought of Julia. The atmosphere of his house enveloped him – quiet and not without dignity, part of a world of lowered voices, and of passions, like Japanese dwarf trees, suppressed for many generations. A familiar world. (*ALMM*, p.175)

Julia's return to Paris, in marked contrast to Horsfield's return home, leads not to a centring but to a decentring of the self. Her life is in fragments, a series of 'disconnected episodes', though looking out her hotel room window she conjures an image of female forlornness with herself (again) as the object of the gaze:

> The houses opposite had long rows of windows, and it seemed to Julia that at each window a woman sat staring mournfully, like a prisoner, straight into her bedroom. (*ALMM*, p.179)

It is an elaborate play of doublings and displacements, which continues as she drifts around Paris. Dreamless at night, she lives daily in a nightmare world of ghosts where she becomes one of the living dead, 'indifferent and cold, like a stone' (*ALMM*, p.188).

It is in this state of total apathy that Julia accidentally encounters Mr Mackenzie again, only to re-enact their separation once more. As with the restaurant scene at the beginning, the focalisation is entirely Mackenzie's as he attempts a small project of self-justification, stopping Julia (when she clearly intends to pass him) on the street and inviting her for a drink in what he sees as a public gesture of forgiveness for her bad behaviour towards him in the restaurant when she had smacked him on the face. Mackenzie even imagines what his friends would say if they could see him, though his complacency is rudely shattered by Julia's failure to appreciate the dimensions of his magnanimity. Julia's only response to his gesture is to ask him for money, exploiting what she now knows to be the only place she occupies in Mackenzie's complacent masculine order. She remains a blank to him and he leaves her sitting drinking a second Pernod.

The final paragraph begins at a distance from Julia, but with characteristic indeterminacy the perspective drifts towards her consciousness by the end:

> The street was cool and full of grey shadows. Lights were beginning to come out in the cafés. It was the hour between dog and wolf, as they say. (*ALMM*, p.191)

Julia may be 'trapped inside a cliché' as Kloepfer suggests [11], but perhaps Rhys is exploiting the idiom '*entre chien et loup*' to position Julia very precisely in a twilight zone, between conformity and domesticity on the one hand and wildness on the other, an exile from both territories.

With its complex system of shifting focalisations and its emphasis on indeterminacy, *After Leaving Mr Mackenzie* is a modernist fiction which repeats Julia's slippage away from the world of conventional discourse through its own strategies of detachment. Rhys is distancing herself from the conventions of romance plot and melodrama through which women's stories have traditionally been told, and which she had used in *Quartet*.[12] Like the modernist women writers whom Rachel Blau Du Plessis discusses, she engages critically with the narratives of heterosexual romance and exposes their falsity, but unlike Woolf, Richardson or Lessing she is unable to find an alternative script for her female protagonists, who are left with nothing.[13] Though the final chapter is called 'Last', there is no single ending, for this novel plays out a series of false endings which are told and retold. There is no heterosexual or maternal union which would give significance to the record of events, the protagonist does not die (though she contemplates drowning herself), and there is throughout a deep scepticism about the value of storytelling itself. This is a novel made of chance encounters in arbitrary circumstances, yet the possibility hovers that events may be structured by an elusive principle that lies beyond 'all the talking and the posturing.' While it is one that neither the protagonist nor the narrator can articulate, the desire for significance is what energises the tellers, who consistently fail to make sense of things.

Julia's failure to make connections between signs and signifieds is at the heart of anxieties of representation in this novel. Is life a riddle whose meaning is undecodable (as Julia believes up to the time of her mother's death), or is it merely (as she comes later to believe), a series of 'disconnected episodes'? Julia's story traps the reader into this process of trying to make sense, only to be left at the end on the borderline between two mutually exclusive possibilities. There are three scenes in the novel which highlight this bafflement of representation: the restaurant scene which George Horsfield sees in its distorted mirror reflection; Julia's memory of her unsuccessful attempt to tell her life story to the woman sculptor; and finally the ambiguous moment of epiphany at her mother's funeral which I have discussed earlier. The restaurant scene which is told first from Mr Mackenzie's perspective, then from George Horsfield's more distanced viewpoint and never from Julia's, opens up the whole question of representation and its relation to meaning. There is no single or essential meaning which can be recovered, and what might have been a dramatic moment of clarification – Julia's heraldic challenge with the glove – falls flat. It is true that Julia is defeated, but it is also true that Mr Mackenzie is not master of the situation either. In this scene framed by the mirror where Horsfield's perspective is the opposite of Julia's (for he is looking at the back of Mr Mackenzie's head and noting the disparity between his pugnacious back view and his 'deliberately picturesque appearance from the front' *ALMM*, p.37), what is imaged is a gesture that might have been 'a caress or a joke' but which is neither. Instead it signals a woman's challenge across the gap of misunderstanding and mutual exploitation in the territory of sexual relationships, and this George Horsfield is not equipped to read.

Rhys appears distrustful here of the efficacy of either visual images or of words to convey the truth, and Julia's repeated attempts to tell her life story always founder. Her most sustained attempt at storytelling is presented as a record of a former failure. In reply to Horsfield's advice that she should 'get out and about and talk to people, not stay by yourself and brood' (*ALMM*, p.49), Julia tries to tell him about her experience with the woman sculptor, not so much in order to tell her story again but rather to prove why 'it doesn't always help to talk to people'. Her account of the woman's reactions of disbelief, interspersed by Horsfield's unspoken masculine irritation at Julia's vagueness, is at once highly critical of the artist's egocentricity and revelatory of Julia's own imprisoning subjectivity. Julia recalls that her narrative had failed either to wrest significance from experience or to convince her listener. Though she had succeeded in framing it in a way that ought to have dramatised her motives to herself, her project was undermined by the Modigliani portrait of a woman on the wall of the artist's studio. This picture, by seeming to absorb and negate the truth of Julia's narrative, merely draws attention to the order of art which mirrors a different kind of truth from that of personal experience:

> It was a beastly feeling I got – that I didn't quite believe myself, either. I thought: "After all, is this true? Did I ever do this?" I felt as if the woman in the picture were laughing at me and saying: "I am more real than you. But at the same time I *am* you. I'm all that matters of you." 'And I felt as if all my life and all myself were floating away from me like smoke and there was nothing to lay hold of – nothing. (*ALMM*, p.53)

Yet Julia's story of the failure of story contains two revelations, one for the reader and one for George Horsfield, though none for herself. We understand why women want to tell their stories, in an attempt to explain and justify their lives. (Julia however takes the urge beyond gender limits by adding in the course of her conversation with Horsfield, 'And of course I forgot that it's always so with everybody, isn't it?', *ALMM*, p.52). We also begin to understand why, by extension, Rhys wants to tell their stories, giving a voice to the women who have been silenced and blamed. Horsfield, despite his masculine reservations about Julia's method of storytelling and his uncertainties about her motives, is forced to recognise the feminine side of the gendered narrative with its glimpse of a woman's pain. The storytelling chapter ends like a modernist short story with Horsfield's moment of epiphany, as always incompletely understood:

> The last thing in his mind before he went to sleep was:
> *Roll me over on my right side,*
> *Roll me over slow;*
> *Roll me over on my right side,*
> *'Cause my left side hurts me so.*
> He did not know where or when he had heard this. For some reason it seemed to him peculiarly applicable to Julia. (*ALMM*, p.56)

Rhys said much later that she 'hated *Mackenzie* and wished she'd never written it'[14], though she did not say why. I suggest that it signals her most painful moments of scepticism about her chosen vocation of writing fiction and her entertainment of the possibility that, like Julia's, her storytelling was a waste of time. Not only did nobody want to hear it, but the very triuumph of narrative artifice was a falsification of lived experience. By adopting the method of multiple shifting perspectives, Rhys shows the inescapable subjectivity in which all her characters are imprisoned; the only common experiences (as the narrative shows) are the most isolating ones of all, those of failure and pain. Separation and exile spell out the dimensions of Julia's feminine displacement, though the focalisation through other characters establishes a wider perspective on confusion and loss as the human condition. Arguably, the narrative representation of the text itself is as baffling, as indecisive, and as riddling as Julia's failed private quest.

# Chapter Four

## *'Starting all over again'*: Voyage in the Dark

> 'She'll be all right,' he said. 'Ready to start all over again in no time, I've no doubt.'
>
> When their voices stopped the ray of light came in again under the door like the last thrust of remembering before everything is blotted out. I lay and watched it and thought about starting all over again. And about being new and fresh. And about mornings, and misty days, when anything might happen. And about starting all over again, all over again . . . [1]

'Again' is the word that echoes and re-echoes at the end of this novel until the narrating consciousness is blotted out. 'Starting all over again' is a borrowed phrase, but not one that is mechanically repeated; instead there is a complex process of repetition which displaces the doctor's complacent social wisdom through the female subject's brief review of the history of her expectations, only to end in her exhausted contemplation of a future that is already predetermined. What 'starting all over again' has reactivated for the last time is the disparity between the discourse of the social order and the protagonist's private counter-discourse which is always at odds, always secret, and finally effectively silenced, as nineteen-year-old Anna Morgan lies emptied out of blood and of words after her bungled abortion.

Rhys first called the novel *Two Tunes*, signifying the double rhythms of the West Indies and England which are insistently repeated in counterpoint to each other within Anna Morgan's consciousness as a white West Indian immigrant. As the site of these conflicting rhythms, represented by the interplay of voices out of two cultures, one remembered and the other presently experienced, Anna is the divided colonial subject, bewildered into silence by the voices of those clashing codes. However, for Anna as a woman there are two other tunes interwoven with the colonial immigrant story, which relate to her gendered narrative. Whereas the social record of her life in England must be read as the story of a girl's entry into prostitution, her own inner tune offers a very different perspective on this old story, composed as it is of childhood memories and romantic fantasies and then of successive betrayals by men, by the English class system, and finally by her own body. The endings of both public and private narratives look very similar in Anna's condition of exhaustion and hopelessness, though her silenced narrative operates as a sustained critique of Englishness and of the patriarchy. Immersed in her own symbolic order, Anna is separated from the English social system within which she exists, and as the novel develops, the issues of colonialism and gender are so closely intermeshed that it is impossible to separate them as the conditions of Anna's disablement.

The second title, *Voyage in the Dark,* offers a revision and a refocusing of Anna's double dislocation, relating her narrative more closely to her West Indian inheritance, for the sea is an important feature of Caribbean geographical and literary space as well as being an historical marker of the notorious Middle Passage of the slave route.[2] Rhys's metaphor of the drifting boat figures another version of that sea journey, positioning Anna as white female Creole subject outside the Caribbean regional order in her wayward passage between two cultures, where she is in danger of being drawn toward that legendary site of becalmed wrecks, the wide Sargasso Sea.

'Starting all over again' is the dreary obverse of Anna's exhilaration at the beginning of the novel, with her excited feeling of 'being born again' into a different way of life on her arrival in England. Though she does not know it, Anna is trapped from the start, telling her story as if 'anything might happen' though it has already been written for her by the imperial texts of colonialism and gender. Anna is inscribed by a whole series of codes related to sex, education, and West Indian cultural history, so that far from being a blank surface on to which male or imperialist fantasies of otherness might be projected, she is already en-gendered/en-cultured. Though she feels constrained to present herself as unreadable or heavily edited text in England, her expectations have been constructed long before her arrival, and she is already disabled by her upbringing from getting on as an independent woman in a metropolitan European context.

The crucial issues here, as in *After Leaving Mr Mackenzie,* are connected with failures of representation as Rhys constructs her version of the feminine in a cross-cultural context in the story of Anna's imprisonment by traditional codes which are emptied of meaning as they are translated from one society to another. Anna fails to adapt to her new environment because she is operating out of a different symbolic order, and all that she learns through her immigrant experience is the full extent of her loss. She is already dispossessed of her West Indian inheritance, and the stages of that betrayal are interwoven in her narrative of memory; in England the loss of her virginity signals her painful initiation into a cycle of sexual exploitation which results in her being finally deprived even of her own story. The narrative which was uniquely her own no longer looks like her own when it is transformed into a social cliché or a lie told through the voices of others. Indeed the parallel problems of colonial and female representation have been spelled out by contemporary post-colonial critics, who argue that the condition of blankness attributed to the 'others' is the result of their being positioned outside the norms of an imperialist tradition and so deprived of their power to signify.[3] Such theorising is exemplified in Anna's failure to figure as a significant subject within English social discourse, where, by definition, hers will be among the 'other stories' relegated to the periphery.

In many ways *Voyage in the Dark* was for Rhys too a matter of 'starting all over again', for the raw material of the narrative is a throwback to the notebooks she kept about the traumatic experience of her first love affair in England. This autobiographical connection gives the changed title of the published novel a new resonance, for, writing of her own life many years later, Rhys referred to herself as 'Le Bateau Ivre', 'always a boat for some reason and in stormy weather too':

> So what with my stormy private life – no, 'stormy' isn't the word. More like one wave after another knocking me against rocks – you see am sticking to being a boat.'[4]

By a process of image association Rhys connects her life with Anna's, indirectly offering a gloss on the title at the very time when she was discussing the possible republication of *Voyage in the Dark* (*JRL*, p.279). In *Smile Please*, written when Rhys was in her eighties, she recalls her love affair with Lancelot Hugh Smith,[5] offering there an account of the novel's evolution over a period of more than twenty years. Of course it is impossible in such a reconstruction to know how much the emotional realities of nearly seventy years earlier are being refracted through the framework of the intervening novel, itself over forty years in the past, but her record offers some of the best evidence we are likely to get about Rhys's writing process. She presents her first sustained attempt at creative writing as having its origins in emotional trauma, remembering it as being outside her conscious control and begun as a personal record:

> I remembered everything that happened to me in the last year and a half. I remembered what he'd said, what I'd felt. I wrote on until late into the night.[6]

After filling three and a half black exercise books, she thought 'there was no more to say', and so she put the books in the bottom of her suitcase and piled her underclothes on top of them. What may well have begun as a therapeutic exercise underwent some surprising transformations, for Rhys kept those notebooks with her in all her travels in Europe after the first World War. They resurfaced again in Paris in 1923 and provided her with an entrée to Ford Madox Ford. Though he was not interested in publishing *Triple Sec*, the first fictional version to be constructed from the notebooks, his influence was important in the novel's evolution, as Rhys claims in 'Leaving School: How I Became a Novelist':

> 'When you go back to London,' he said another day in his quiet voice. 'I am never going to live in London again. Never.'
> 'Oh yes you will and you'll want to write about it as you knew it.

> Then Triple Sec or whatever you call it will come in very useful, so don't tear it up or anything silly like that.'
> He was quite right.[7]

*Voyage in the Dark* evolved as a multilayered narrative of memory twelve years later, when, having returned to London, Rhys recalled that conversation with Ford in Paris:

> Suddenly the book I wanted to write and even its title [*Two Tunes*?] was clear in my head and I hurried back to start.
> It is the only book I have ever written quickly, easily, and with confidence.
> And it ran into trouble at once.[8]

Rhys is here referring to the wrangle over the ending of *Voyage in the Dark*, which she finally had to agree, under pressure from Michael Sadleir at Constable's, to change in order to get it published.[9] Instead of Anna's death as the result of her abortion, Rhys rewrote it with Anna surviving:

> Oh, give the girl a chance. So I spent several very gloomy weeks trying to think of two or three paragraphs that would not spoil the book. Trying to give the girl a chance.[10]

She gives a more emotional account of her resistance and defeat in a letter to Evelyn Scott, where she complains about the 'mutilation' that she is being forced to commit.[11] *Voyage in the Dark* was published by Constable in October 1934, to be met with only grudging respect from reviewers who still disapproved of her subject matter: 'Within the limits of her subject, Miss Rhys has done a very nearly perfect job.'[12] As a footnote, when Deutsch republished the novel in 1967, Rhys chose to leave the ending as it was, for by then, as she wrote to Oliver Stoner, she wished to use some of the material of the original ending in her autobiography.[13] Diana Athill, her editor at Deutsch, noted that Rhys did not tell her that she had found the typescript of the original ending, though Rhys did send it to Selma Vaz Dias who was working on a radio adaptation of the novel in 1963.[14]

Arguably the close correspondences between autobiography and novel merely highlight the play of difference between genres, to which Rhys frequently drew attention: 'a novel has to have shape, and life doesn't have any,'[15] and 'a girl like that would be bewildered from start to finish.'[16] The fictional text cannot be converted back into autobiography, and even *Smile Please* is another later text.The long gestation of the novel blurs further the relation between the writer and her protagonist. Indeed, the very fact that Anna cannot even get a letter written to Walter separates her from the novelist ( though the reader's curiosity is provoked as to how close Anna's unpunctuated outburst of feeling in her unfinished letter to Walter was to Rhys's first record of her affair in those original notebooks, the location of which I have not been able to discover. Is Anna's letter Rhys's inscription of her repressed diary material?) Anna is a fictional construct positioned and imprisoned by the narrative with its exposure of the imprisoning codes of gender and colonialism. She lives or dies according to the dictates of the story. Anna may be a silenced subject but Rhys is not; and her adoption of the first person narrative is a brilliant response to the challenge of writing about a confused and increasingly speechless young woman, a response which defies the very silencing to which Anna is forced to submit. This multivoiced text records and interprets in ways that Anna could not do for herself, just as it demonstrates the impossibility of Anna's finding an effective form of intervention, let alone resistance, in the English social system.

The novel begins as the monologue of a dislocated colonial subject, ungendered for the first two paragraphs and curiously predating, with its images of theatricality and redemption, the duplicities of immigrant experience which Salman Rushdie records at the beginning of his *Satanic Verses*. Though his protagonists fall from the sky and Anna does not, her entry into England is equally traumatic:

> It was as if a curtain had fallen, hiding everything I had ever known. It was almost like being born again. The colours were different, the smells different, the feeling things gave you right down inside yourself was different. Not just the difference between heat, cold; light, darkness; purple, grey. But a difference in the way I was frightened and the way I was happy. I didn't like England at first. I couldn't get used to the cold . . . It was funny, but that was what I thought about more than anything else – the smell of the streets

> and the smells of frangipanni and lime juice and cinnamon and cloves, and sweets made of ginger and syrup, and incense after funerals or Corpus Christi processions, and the patients standing outside the surgery next door, and the smell of the sea-breeze and the different smell of the land-breeze. (*VID*, pp.7–8)

Though 'Two Tunes' epitomises the opening of this paragraph, by its end measured counterpoint has given way to a rhapsody celebrating a vanished West Indian world. That native culture of the marketplace is described so vividly that the lost place of 'home' assumes all the vitality of presence, shutting out England entirely. This opening establishes an oppositional relationship between the speaker's past and present, where one culture excludes or denies the other:

> Sometimes it was as if I were back there and as if England were a dream. At other times England was the real thing and out there was the dream, but I could never fit them together. (*VID*, p.8)

Caught between two different signifying systems with a 'curtain' separating them, the narrator's consciousness appears to be radically split, where a total immersion in one dimension of experience precludes any participation in the other. The basic structure of the novel is built on that premise, with narrrative blocks of remembered West Indian experience juxtaposed with blocks of English experience, demonstrating Rhys's stated intention to write a novel about the dissolution of time within human consciousness:

> The big idea – well I'm blowed if I can be sure what it is. Something to do with time being an illusion I think. I mean that the past exists – side by side with the present, not behind it; that what was – is.[17]

Yet precisely because the narrator's consciousness contains both 'tunes' a pure dualism cannot be sustained. Memories will intrude through imaginative association with the present, so that the initial opposition is destabilised and becomes as much a play of difference within the subject as between the subject and the external order. By the end of the first part (or movement) of the novel, the counterpoint structure of narrative blocks set against each other has developed into a more complex pattern of interweaving between memory and present time, till in the final (fourth) part the pattern re-echoes the opening configuration. However, there is the vital difference that the narrating consciousness has moved to the other side of the curtain, submerged in the order of memory in her hallucinatory return 'home'. No longer are there two separate tunes, but instead a scrambling of voices and rhythms in the narrative of a fragmented silenced subject.[18] Rhys's own comment on this complex structure is typically dismissive though entirely accurate in its reductive way: 'Perhaps I was simply trying to describe a girl going potty.'[19]

It is when the 'English tune' is introduced in the third paragraph that the gender of the narrating subject is revealed, for this is Anna's story of her experiences as an immigrant woman. It begins bleakly enough, drained of emotion in a scenario of dreary repetition:

> After a while I got used to England and I liked it all right; I got used to everything except the cold and that the towns we went to always looked so exactly alike. (*VID*, p.8)

Again a curtain falls with appropriate theatricality across the narrative of the life of a chorus girl, where two tunes are developed in a contrapuntal pattern, though this time there is no interweaving between them for the Harlot's Progress of the main text bears little relation to the story told from Anna's perspective. Penniless and socially displaced, Anna drifts from her shiftless life on the stage through an unhappy love affair into prostitution, in a career that reads like one of the clichés of social and fictional discourse about male–female relations. Indeed her destiny is already written in the text for her, and for the reader, on the third page. In one of an endless succession of furnished rooms, Anna is lying on the sofa reading Zola's *Nana*, or rather not reading it but feeling both excited and frightened by the picture of a woman sitting on the knee of a man in evening dress and by the look of the 'dark, blurred words going on endlessly' (*VID*, p.9). It is there like a prophecy that she cannot decipher but it outlines a script of social and gender determinism as implacable as that metaphysical order spelled out in her childhood as the word of God: 'As it was in the beginning, is now, and ever shall be, world without end' (*VID*, p.41).

Against this social construction of female destiny, runs Anna's subtext of fantasy which derives from a symbolic order of childhood anterior to adulthood and to England, associated with Dominica and Anna's vanished mothers. This maternal principle may be read as the Kristevan 'semiotic' as Deborah Kelly Kloepfer argues in her discussion of *Voyage in the Dark*,[20] though that remembered state of happiness is deconstructed through Anna's successive memories of her young mother's funeral, her rejection by the black cook Francine, the disapproval of her English step mother, and her feeling of estrangement in Dominica. Anna's narrative operates within a complex economy of loss as her consciousness hovers around that central absence which includes the nurturing figure of Francine and the childhood place from which she has been exiled. Anna's deepest desire is to return to the remembered/imagined state of plenitude before her experience of self-division, and it is this impossible desire that she pursues, translated into the always inappropriate and approximate forms of romantic fantasy.

It is fascinating that in this narrative of a prostitute's career told by a woman ('I bet you a man writing a book about a tart tells a lot of lies one way and another', *VID*, p.10) there is an almost total absence of female sexual desire. Instead of the voracious female sexuality of *Nana* which obsessed Zola's imagination, where in Peter Brooks's phrase 'the body of the prostitute is the meeting point of Eros and Commerce,'[21] Rhys's prostitutes do not confuse the two. The erotic is drained out of what is seen as a commercial transaction, as Maudie's advice to Anna suggests, 'The thing with men is to get everything you can out of them and not care a damn' (*VID*, p.38). In the heterosexual economy of this novel the emphasis is on mutual exploitation and contempt. Not only is the male attitude towards women like Anna or Maudie or Laurie encoded in dismissive references to them always in the plural as 'you girls', but this is paralleled in stringent feminine criticism of the predictabilities of male behaviour. The men too are referred to in the plural and with some animosity,'I hated them both' (*VID*, p.13).

Though Anna is drawn into the traditional script of the

chorus girl's affair with the gentleman when she becomes involved with Walter Jeffries, 'a man from the city', it is typical of her naïve romanticism that she should see her first dinner date with him in London as a scene from a novelette:

> It was a pity about my clothes, but anyway they were black. 'She wore black. Men delighted in that sable colour, or lack of colour. 'A man called 'Coronet' wrote that, or was it a man called 'A Peer'? (*VID*, p.22)

It is not surprising that she should be shocked when the explicitly sexual nature of this transaction is made plain after dinner, where the situation degenerates into a wry comedy of mutual incomprehension. However, the narrative shifts to something much less familiar as it registers the complex sexual dynamics of this interchange and Anna's yearning to close the gap between romantic fantasy and reality: 'If it could go back and be just as it was before it happened and then happen differently' (*VID*, p.23). There is an interesting link here, in terms of writing in the feminine between Anna's wish and Virginia Woolf's identification of the demands of George Eliot's heroines, which is codified by Nancy K.Miller as 'this demand of the heroine for something else . . . the extravagant wish for a story that would turn out differently'.[22]

However, this story is not about difference but about sameness, and Anna intuitively recognises that her story is about to be taken out of her hands when, sitting alone in the bedroom having refused Walter's advances, she stares at herself in the mirror: 'It was as if I were looking at somebody else' (*VID*, p.23).This disjunction between her body and her image is the first sign of that dispersal of herself which Anna will suffer as she is drawn into a story that is at odds with her deepest desires, but she cannot articulate these desires beyond her yearning for difference. When Walter Jeffries sends her 'a big bunch of violets' and twenty pounds, she eagerly allows herself to be cast into the role of child or doll in order to re-enter her own fantasy narrative:

> This is a beginning. Out of this warm room that smells of fur I'll go to all the lovely places I've ever dreamt of. This is the beginning. (*VID*, p.28)

Echoing her earlier sense of being born again, it shows an airy optimism which is gradually emptied of meaning as the story develops. Whatever her dreams, Anna cannot escape the social reality within which her relationship with Walter is situated, as the landlady's ungracious remarks make plain: 'I don't want no tarts in my house, so now you know' (*VID*, p.30).

Anna's account of the affair between herself and Walter highlights nothing so much as the unbridgeable gaps between them. As the story develops through blocks of Anna's interior monologue, interspersed with patches of dialogue in the daily context of their relationship, we perceive behind this a subtext of desire which is connected with Anna's history of loss and dislocation. Whereas Walter's behaviour conforms to the traditional male plot of a conventional affair with a very shy and sexually inexperienced girl, Anna recasts him within her private narrative into a protective role where his sexuality is almost obliterated. She transforms him from lover to mother, or at least into a surrogate for the sheltering maternal principle, so that when their affair ends Anna will conflate his betrayal with all the other betrayals of her childhood. One clear sign of her private narrative is Anna's refrain, 'Adieu', which is first of all associated with Francine's song, 'Adieu, sweetheart, adieu' (*VID*, p.32) and her memories of sailing away from her island home, and then later assimilated to the loss of Walter. Anna's symbolic order is closer to an infantile dynamics of dependence than it ever is to sexual desire.

When she does go to bed with Walter, all Anna registers is the warmth of his body, and in her secret dialogue with herself she comes close to finding her private language of desire:

> When I got into bed there was warmth coming from him and I got close to him. *Of course you've always known , always remembered, and then you forget so utterly, except that you've always known it. Always – how long is always?* (*VID*, p.37)[23]

Anna's is an impossible desire for a return to the preverbal phase of primal physical intimacy which is remembered at the back of consciousness. Her sexual initiation reads not like a voyage of sexual discovery but more like a repudiation of the concept of sexual difference. Indeed, there is no description of the sexual act – only a gap in the text between paragraphs – and then Anna's comment, 'I thought it had been just like the girls said, except that I hadn't known it would hurt so much' (*VID*, p.33).

The radical difference in frames of reference between Anna and Walter is signalled in odd interruptive moments where the seams between their different scripts show through, like the moment when Anna responds to Walter's conventional male gesture of putting money in her purse:

> I meant to say, 'What are you doing?' But when I went up to him instead of saying, 'Don't do that,' I said, 'All right, if you like – anything you like, any way you like.' And I kissed his hand.
> 'Don't,' he said. 'It's I who ought to kiss your hand, not you mine.'
> I felt miserable suddenly and utterly lost. 'Why did I do that?' I thought. (*VID*, pp.38–9)

Anna herself cannot account for her sudden gesture of submission, though the hidden configurations of her narrative begin to emerge when, on another occasion, she tries to tell Walter about her life in the West Indies, because she wanted to make him understand what it had been like. The thematics of gender and colonialism intermesh here in Anna's incomprehensible remarks about the name of the girl on the slave list which she remembers seeing at Constance estate, 'Maillotte Boyd, aged 18, mulatto, house servant' (*VID*, p.53). Again the gaps between discourses show plainly, as Anna's tale of remembered Caribbean images is systematically rejected by Walter as being outside his frame of reference:

> The tropics would be altogether too lush for me, I think.' 'But it isn't lush,' I said. 'You're quite wrong. It's wild and a bit sad sometimes. You might as well say the sun's lush.' (*VID*, pp.54)

As well as indicating his Englishness, Walter's comments indirectly suggest the male association of 'woman' with everything that is wild and excessive, recalling Ford's remarks about Rhys herself in his *Left Bank* Preface. Walter terminates Anna's earnest fragmented narrative by insisting on returning to the conventional script of their relationship: 'You sound a bit tight,' he said. 'Well, let's go upstairs, you rum child, you rum little devil.' (*VID*, p.55)

Anna's story has been effectively silenced, yet her secret dialogue goes on as they lie together in bed, with her thoughts of sin and transgression and the recurrence of the slave girl's name: '*Maillotte Boyd, aged 18. Maillotte Boyd, aged 18 . . . But I like it like this. I don't want it any other way but this*' (*VID*, p.56). Two important thematic strands are signalled here: Anna's Creole inheritance of white historical guilt and the intimate connections between sex and slavery, for Anna's only representation of female sexuality is the figure of the black slave girl in her position of dependence and submission to her master. Later, at the end of her affair, Anna will draw a ferociously explicit analogy between the politics of colonialism and gender when she recalls the indigenous Caribs and their near-extinction at the hands of European colonisers in the late seventeenth and early eighteenth centuries. There is also an extra-textual dimension suggested by Anna's words, for they recall Rhys's Mr Howard narrative of the adolescent colonial girl and the elderly Englishman, where she too figured as a naked slave girl: 'If anyone were to offer to save me I would refuse. If anyone were to say Shall I save you I would answer no'.[24]

Within the script of Anna's romantic fantasy her acquiescence in the hierarchy of sexual domination and submission is inevitable. Yet her multiple frames of colonial reference are no more viable within the order of English social discourse than are her infantile yearnings for her vanished mother within the order of adult sexuality. What Anna desires is outside the boundaries of possibility; her slave girl submissiveness is devalued by her lover and her childishness is parodied by his cousin Vincent's constant references to her as 'my infantile Anna.' As she discovers, there is no space in language or in cultural practice for what she desires, just as there is no escape either from patriarchal structures or from biological bondage to her own femaleness.

The narrative of Anna's love affair is interrupted by her satirical account of a confrontation in London with her English stepmother Hester, where the gendered narrative is displaced by the antagonisms of a colonial encounter. Hester is a self-appointed representative of English cultural supremacy, with her 'English lady's voice, with a sharp cutting edge to it. Now that I've spoken you can hear that I'm a lady. I have my doubts about you' (*VID*, p.57). Ostensibly their meeting at Hester's hotel is to discuss a letter from Anna's maternal uncle in Dominica in which he accuses his sister-in-law of robbing Anna of her West Indian inheritance. In the conflicting narratives of accusation and self-righteous justification, there is demonstrably no common ground, for Hester had hated the West Indies and regarded it as her imperial mission to give Anna a 'real chance' by bringing her to England. The gap between English and colonial points of view is emblematised in the word 'gentleman':

> 'Your uncle is not a gentleman and I shall tell him so.'
> 'Oh, he won't mind that,' I said. I couldn't help laughing. Thinking of Uncle Bo getting a letter which began 'Dear Ramsay, You are not a gentleman . . . '(*VID*, p.64)

Anna's dissent from Hester's values provokes a series of derogatory comments on her Creole background – aspersions on Anna's mixed ancestry and on her voice ('Exactly like a nigger you talked – and still do', *VID*, p.65). In Hester's narrative, Anna figures as the cast-out other who fails to come up to British standards: 'My conscience is quite clear. I always did my best for you and I never got any thanks for it (*VID*, p.65).

The issue of money is the ostensible point of this discussion, but Hester's indignation over the question of Anna's colonial inheritance only masks the sexual issue, as is indicated by Anna's unspoken monologue which runs in ironic counterpoint beneath their conversation:

> I sat there. I didn't know what to say. There wasn't anything to say. I kept on wondering whether she would ask me what I was living on. 'What is Purity? For Thirty-five Years the Answer has been Bourne's Cocoa.' Thirty-five years . . . Fancy being thirty-five years old. What is Purity? For Thirty-five Thousand Years the Answer has been . . . (*VID*, p.59)

Within the decorum imposed by her stepmother, any question of Anna's present source of income is noisily silenced, and Anna is dismissed. The only visible sign of her resistance is her refusal to join in the ritual of taking tea with Hester before she leaves.

Now that she is marooned in England and cut off by lack of money from any possibility of returning to Dominica, Anna's interior monologue circles back via all that was unsaid in her meeting with Hester to the memory of her traumatic entry into womanhood. The day Anna's first menstruation began marks the end of unselfconsciousness as she is forced to submit to what in Lacanian terms would be called the symbolic order. As Juliet Mitchell comments, 'The symbolic is the point of organisation, the point where sexuality is constructed as meaning, where what was heterogeneous, what was not symbolised, becomes organised, becomes created around two poles, masculine and not-masculine: feminine.'[25] For Anna the inflections of difference are not only gendered but racial, for they include her sudden sharp awareness of separation from Francine at the same time as she herself is classified as a white woman:

> But I knew that of course she disliked me too because I was white: and that I would never be able to explain to her that I hated being white. Being white and getting like Hester, and all the things you get – old and sad and everything. I kept thinking: 'No . . . No . . . No.' And I knew that day that I'd started to grow old and nothing could stop it. (*VID*, p.72)

Despite her desperate refusals of the growing up process and all that it signifies, Anna knows that she is trapped by her body into a set of cultural prescriptions spelled out by Hester and which make her feel so suffocated that she remembers wanting to die.

The crucial importance of the beginning of Anna's gendered narrative is emphasised by its positioning, intercalated into her story about Walter and framed by the words 'That was when it was sad', which occur at the end of the preceding chapter and at the beginning of the one following. In both cases the words refer to the undercurrents of fear which run beneath Anna's state of being in love, for to be a woman is to be at risk and subject to an order prescribed by others. According to the social discourse there is no future in Anna's relationship with Walter, as she herself knows:

> When it was sad was when you woke up at night and thought about being alone and that everybody says the man's bound to get tired . . . Everybody says, 'Get on.' . . . Get on or get out, they say. Get on or get out. (*VID*, p.74)

Though Anna tries to avoid the reality of her situation, preferring to believe that 'this was the best way to live in the world, because anything might happen' (*VID*, p.75), she is constantly reminded of it by the voices of others – by her friend Maudie, by Vincent with his patronising arrogance, and by Vincent's French girl-friend Germaine with her savage criticism of Englishmen's 'scorn and loathing for the female' (*VID*, p.81). Her dreads and intuitions run ahead of her conscious knowledge, coding themselves in fragments of memory in a technique of displacement which bears striking similarities to Freud's dreamwork. When the letter from Vincent arrives to announce the ending of the relationship with Walter, Anna's response to the sight of the unfamiliar handwriting is an apparently random recall of a childhood episode when she had been terrified by the sight of her uncle's false teeth which had looked to her like long yellow tusks. While she is wondering what the letter has to do with false teeth, the memory develops its own intricate associative patterns via bizarre images of piano keys, her father's words about 'Hiraeth' being the Welsh word for grief, and his comment, 'I've met some Englishmen . . . who were monkeys too' (*VID*, p.95). It is this image around which Anna's mind circles in her last meeting with Walter, suggesting her blame of him along with her awareness that she has no voice through which to make an effective appeal against his decision. Indeed, she feels trapped into voicelessness as if she were trying to speak from under water.

The relationship is turned by Walter into a commercial transaction conducted through the intermediaries of his cousin and his lawyer in a way which her friend Laurie recognises as typical, but which Anna interprets very differently. She feels it as a breakage within herself:

> But what happens if you don't hope any more, if your back's broken? What happens then?' (*VID*, p.130)

This metaphor of physical wounding is the sign of Anna's splitting apart. No longer will she talk about beginnings, but instead she withdraws into memory and fantasy as her only means of escape from an oppressive social reality where 'the shapes of the slices of meat were the same, and the way the cabbage was heaped was the same, and all the houses outside in the street were the same – all alike, all hideously stuck together' (*VID*, p.103).

The rest of her story is all aftermath to her affair with Walter, as the words 'never:' and 'never again' resound in the subtext beneath the superficial gaiety of her life. Compressed as it is into less than half the novel, it charts Anna's increasing indifference to the social narratives imposed on her by others as she blanks out their voices to listen instead to her internal narrative composed of the voices of her vanished West Indian past.

In the second and third sections of the novel the blocks of gendered and colonial narrative are no longer easily separable. Like the English terraced houses, everything is 'hideously stuck together' as the antagonisms of class, gender and culture become more explicit. As her prospects darken, Anna begins to adopt a savagely Darwinian perspective on the fight for survival. She transforms Ethel Matthews, the English masseuse who befriends her at the lodging house, into an insect with clever eyes: 'Feelers grow when feelers are needed and claws when claws are needed and cunning when cunning is needed' (*VID*, p.107). With this image recalling the swarming woodlice of her childhood, Anna places Ethel as 'one of the ones with beastly lives' (*VID*, p.26), and though Ethel's ambiguous friendship, sympathetic yet wary of 'dirty foreigners', offers Anna the possibility of a different future from the prostitute's career, it is in essential respects the same. Ethel too is a female victim whose only means of survival is to enter into complicity with the male 'idiots and brutes' who have the money. When the mask of cheerful endurance slips, Ethel spells out the parallels between their situations as women without money, and although Anna refuses to respond to her threats and deliberately distances herself, her habitual associative processes lead her directly to the focus of her alienation in the jade bracelet given to her by Walter:

> It felt warm and comforting against my hand and I gripped it and looked at it but I couldn't remember the word. (*VID*, p.147)

When she does remember the word, the warmth and comfort are savagely turned inside out:

> It felt warm and comforting because I knew I could hit somebody pretty hard with it. And I remembered the word. Knuckle-duster. (*VID*, p.148)

Standing outside Walter's house all those evenings ago, Anna had felt that 'Something about the darkness of the streets has a meaning' (*VID*, p.57), and now she has begun to discover the meaning of being an outsider. She has learned that a woman alone needs weapons not only against casual male insults but also against the law itself where the policeman stares at her 'like a damned baboon – a fair baboon, too, worse than a dark one every time' (*VID*, p.148). In that remark, which recalls her father's words, 'I've met some Englishmen who were monkeys too,' is encoded Anna's bitter revision of her colonial image of England, now focused on her failed love affair with an Englishman. Recalling an advertisement for English biscuits 'as Fresh in the Tropics as in the Motherland' and its picture of a girl and boy in a walled English garden, Anna comments, 'But it was the wall that mattered' (*VID*, p.149). Anna, like Rhys herself, suffers from 'disappointed love' in her relations with England and the English.

When Laurie reappears in the company of two Americans ('I've been showing them round, I can tell you,' (*VID*, p.115), Anna allows herself to be drawn into that narrative despite the warning of one of the Americans, 'Don't you know she's a tart?' *VID*, p.127. The first time Anna goes out with Laurie and her companions she is wearing a borrowed dress of Laurie's which doesn't fit properly. Indeed nothing fits, and in her displacement Anna retraces in memory the different roads she has travelled – in England as a chorus girl and earlier back home along the road that led to the house on the old plantation:

> Then do you turn to the right or the left? . . . It took three hours to get to Constance Estate. It was as long as a life sometimes. (*VID*, p.151)

Indeed, it will take Anna quite that long to get back there again in memory. When she resurfaces out of her reverie into ordinary life, she retains fragments like the negro song, *Campdown Racecourse*, and when shortly after this she begins her journey along the road to prostitution by going to bed with Joe, one of Laurie's Americans, her wry commentary on the proceedings takes up the rhythms of the remembered song in her implicit linkage between plantations, slavery and female sexuality. Though Anna naïvely insists that 'Somebody won on the bay,' she is reminded by Joe of the rules of the game, 'Nobody wins. Don't worry. Nobody wins' (*VID*, p.129).

Anna's career has all the marks of repetitiousness which are endemic to narratives of prostitutes' lives, though it lacks the usual sexual interest, for it seems as if, after her failed affair, Anna is sexually anaesthetised. While her blankness conforms to male fantasies of female passivity, it is at the same time Anna's way of resisting this construction of herself by refusing to participate fully in the sexual games prescribed by masculine society where a girl like her is nothing more than an object of entertainment:

> I picked up a girl in London and she . . . Last night I slept with a girl who' . . . That was me.
> Not 'girl' perhaps. Some other word, perhaps. Never mind. (*VID*, p.157)

If men see her as doll-like and without identity, Anna in her turn denies them their individuality, so that a succession of men becomes an undifferentiated 'he'. Anna develops a spiteful contempt for her clients: she laughs at the man whose foot gets burned with boiling water, just as later she strikes out at the man with a bandaged wrist. Prostitution is to Anna a savage game where nobody wins.

In the end Anna is caught, for the doll's body is also a

woman's body and Anna finds she is pregnant. She is reminded of the reality of her femaleness in the most traumatic ways, through an unwanted pregnancy followed by an abortion. At this crisis point where the 'fantastic' becomes the 'inevitable', Anna once again tries to blur the distinction by retreating in memory and dream, finding her escape route in the words of the song, *Connais-tu le Pays*, which she had refused to play for a client just a few minutes before everything started heaving up and down 'like seasickness, only worse' (*VID*, p.162). That song opens the way into her secret remembered life as she recalls its being sung at home by old Miss Jackson, Colonel Jackson's illegitimate daughter , 'yes illegitimate poor old thing but such a charming woman really' (*VID*, p.162). So begins a strain of memory which bears within it the traces of Anna's present anxieties translated from gendered into Caribbean terms, where colonisation is the common denominator. Her memories of home become more threatening with their haunted mountains and zombies merging into her dream of a sea voyage and a dead boy bishop smiling cruelly in his coffin, as complex parallels are woven into a deterministic pattern. Anna's dream ends with her vision of estrangement, where home itself has become both strange and unreachable:

> I was still trying to walk up the deck and get ashore . . . and when I woke up everything was still heaving up and down. (*VID*, p.165)

As Anna attempts to elude the biological consequences of the sexual game, she is forced to confront the twin realities of male economic power and male indifference, bearing witness to Susan Gubar's remark that 'women have had to experience cultural scripts in their lives by suffering them in their bodies.'[26] Though Laurie can give Anna advice about a woman who would do an abortion, Anna needs the kind of money that only Walter can provide, and in order to get it she has to submit to the humiliation of being patronised once again by Vincent 'with his look like a high smooth unclimbable wall' (*VID*, p.172). With another male voice ringing in her ears, reminding her that life is nothing but a huge and ironic joke, Anna goes to the abortionist's flat. But the joke turns sour for Anna. Far from the abortion's being 'nothing to make a fuss about' as Vincent had assured her, she emerges from her visit to Mrs Robinson with a conviction of her own mortality, afraid of crossing the street and afraid of the people passing because she felt that she was dying.

There are two endings to the novel: the original Part Four where Anna dies; and the published one, half its length, where Anna survives the bungled abortion. Both versions have a similar form as Anna's interior monologue runs backwards from present crisis into childhood memories of home. However, the original ending presents a more sustained retreat into that earlier symbolic order, and Anna dies there as the hallucinations of memory give way to blackness and silence:

> And the concertina music stopped and it was so still so still and lovely just like before you go to sleep and it stopped and there was the ray of light along the floor like the last thrust of remembering before everything is blotted out and blackness comes . . . [27]

(This ending is close to Antoinette's last dream in *Wide Sargasso Sea* when she leaps into her vision of a vanished past which is itself death-dealing.) Arguably the original ending is more shocking in its silent challenge to the complacent social assumptions that the abortion will be 'all right', but the revised version is more ironical, for Anna's survival appears to validate those same assumptions. Either way, it is Anna who is the loser.

The revised ending begins not in the past but in the present as Anna lies on the bed bleeding copiously, though already she has begun drifting back to the past, as her description of the room obliquely indicates:

> The room was nearly dark but there was a long yellow ray coming in under the door from the light in the passage. I lay and watched it. I thought, 'I'm glad it happened when nobody was here because I hate people.' (*VID*, p.183)

Seemingly naturalistic, this description focuses back through layers of memory, via the first time Walter came to see her, to one of the rooms at home on an occasion when she had had fever and saw the ' yellow light [which] came in through the slats and lay on the floor in bars' (*VID*, p.31).Then she had lain watching a cockroach, and Francine had come in to comfort her, but now she is attended only by the cleaning woman and Laurie, neither of whom wants to be 'mixed up with a thing like this.' The two women's voices together with sensations of giddiness and fears of falling through the bed constitute the mesh of signifiers through which Anna traces her way back home, into memories of the masquerade in Passion Week and the horse ride up to Constance Estate.

However something has gone wrong, for Anna finds that she is shut out from that vibrant vanished life. Her memory of the lost place throws up a different series of images which are the negative of the rhapsodic opening paragraph of the novel. Instead of undifferentiated relationship to that Caribbean community, Anna now sees everything from a white perspective where the illusion of harmony changes to a vision of that same community deeply divided by racial hostilities. Anna is an outsider watching the black masquerade from behind the slats of the jalousies. As the English voices of her father, her stepmother and her uncles and aunts interweave with the music of the concertina-man and the triangle-man and the man who played the chak-chak, the carnival becomes a nightmare of noise and threatening masks. Though the masks would at first seem to image mindless chaos, *'a mask Father said with an idiot behind it'* (*VID*, p.184), the focus soon sharpens into a much more specific image of racial antagonism and fear. Anna recalls the masks the black women wore, with their crude imitations of European faces painted on them, and especially their two mouths, *'a little red heart-shaped mouth and under the mouth another slit so that they could put their tongues out at you'* (*VID*, p.185). The carnival masks come to figure the blacks' parodic relation to white society where the mimic surface only partially conceals the subversive mocking other, to the white Creole child caught within the conflicting codes of the Caribbean colonial system.

Anna too is caught between memory and her present bodily sensations, so that in her dreamlike monologue the noises of the carnival become scrambled with her feelings of giddiness, merging into her remembered horseback ride:

> *I heard the concertina-music playing behind me all the time and the noise of the people's feet dancing – the street was in a greenish shadow* (*VID*, p.186)

But when she gets there the green forest has vanished, and

Constance Estate is only a ruined landscape, *'a place where nobody is a place full of stones where nobody is'*, deserted but for ghosts and shadows in the moonlight. If she was afraid of otherness before, now Anna is afraid of falling into nothingness, *'nothing can save me now but still I clung desperately with my knees feeling very sick'* (*VID*, p.187).

She finally speaks out from her hallucination: 'I fell,' I said. 'I fell for a hell of a long time then' and Laurie takes up her words, turning them into a lie about the abortion:

> 'Tell him you had a fall,' she said. 'That's all you've got to say . . . '
> 'Oh, so you had a fall, did you?' the doctor said. (*VID*, p.187)

The voices of Laurie and the doctor are the voices of worldly wisdom which drown Anna's voice, obliterating her story in the clichés of their social text.

Yet there is a sense in which Anna's damaged body refuses this social silencing, for her real text is written in blood. Deprived of will, Anna writes a red incoherent text of the female body's pain as she haemorrhages uncontrollably. Actually the analogy between bloodstained sheets and printed page is clearer in the unpublished version, when the cleaning woman declares,

> 'Look at that mattress . . . What about that mattress?
> There's going to be a row about this.'[28]

In the published ending all that she says is, 'It ought to be stopped' (*VID*, p.157). Finally, it is within Anna's body that the double narratives are knitted together, as Anna's memories of the Caribbean carnival and the horse-ride are stimulated by her giddiness and longing. The lush remembered place of Constance Estate is transformed into a ruined Gothic landscape as her body is drained of life.

In the end, there is nowhere for Anna to inhabit except the text itself. The final paragraph registers this emptying out of personality and the terrible forlornness of her loss where, deprived of anything except a textual existence that is almost over, Anna is condemned to repeat the doctor's words just as she echoes the earlier words of her own story. So the printed words of Zola's *Nana* merge with God's text of immutable order and the social texts of class, gender and colonialism, effectively silencing Anna's secret narrative of desire as she recedes into an endless repetition of what has already been said and already been written.

# Chapter Five

# *'No pride, no name, no face, no country'*: Good Morning, Midnight

I have no pride – no pride, no name, no face, no country.
I don't belong anywhere. Too sad, too sad. . .[1].

While this quotation would seem emblematic of woman as Other, existing only in negative relation to the male symbolic order, it also points quite specifically to a state of crisis within the female subject, just as it prefigures the silencing of Rhys's voice as a novelist for a period of over twenty years. It is this crisis of subjectivity and its implications for the representation of the feminine within a modernist novel that I propose to discuss, for Rhys is exploring new territory here as her protagonist, Sasha Jansen, moves into those dark forbidden spaces imaged in Emily Dickinson's poetry and which contemporary feminist critics propose as the distinctive site for women's writing.[2] As a document of female modernism, *Good Morning, Midnight* acknowledges 'the power of the (male/ 'universal') space in which it cannot avoid to some extent operating'[3], yet it deliberately situates itself as a critique of male modernist representations of the city, of social history and above all, of their representations of women. Sasha is neither Molly Bloom nor the hyacinth girl nor the typist in *The Waste Land*, yet she has enough in common with all three to be able to expose the romanticism and the misogyny of these masculine constructions. Writing against *Ulysses* and *The Waste Land* and showing Sasha prostituting her literary talents as a ghost writer of fairytales ('This story . . . is an allegory', *GMM*, p.166), Rhys has herself written an allegory of the situation of the modern woman writer.

The dark spaces signalled by the title and the epigraph from Dickinson's poem point to Rhys's double project here. The brilliant oxymoron is the perfect figure for her protagonist's spiritual journey towards oblivion, while the unusually specific literary allusion relates her novel to female literary tradition and to what has been called Emily Dickinson's 'politics of refusal.'[4] Yet there is a significant difference of positioning; while Dickinson's 'metaphoric identification with darkness' arguably marks 'a politics of acceptance, even assertion, of her position as a woman writer,'[5] Rhys's is more obviously a 'politics of exclusion' as she sees herself rejected by the patriarchal literary world. Unlike Dickinson, she does not see darkness as a positive choice; the space that she and her protagonist are forced into is the only exit from their marginalised position of beggary and fight for survival. The conditions of being a woman and being a woman writer coalesce here, as a Black Exercise Book entry suggests:

> If you only knew what it was to be a woman without any money even now. May the Lord protect us. It's alright if you're stupid. Yet who would deliberately wish to be stupid? Not one. No one would wish to be blind no one would wish to be stupid.[6]

Sasha tries to be both blind and stupid. Indeed she is accused of stupidity by the Englishman Mr Blank in the story ('This woman is the biggest fool I've ever met in my life, *GMM*, p.27), as she was also accused by two English male reviewers[7]. The trouble is that she is far from stupid: however hard she tries for blankness and indifference, her 'sale cerveau' (*GMM*, p.187) continues to function, forcing her to remember when she would prefer to forget, to make connections, to launch savage social criticisms, and to indulge in painful self parody. Sasha's is a damaged psyche and her relationship to the external world is disturbed, but she is not a blank surface; instead, there is always the repressed subtext of her personal history which erupts into and disrupts her carefully constructed automaton image.

Yet it is true that there is a radically different subject construction in this novel from that adopted by Rhys anywhere else. Repudiating notions of essentialism and the idea of a 'real self', she presents neither an unstable subject like Marya or Julia, nor a split subject like Anna, but a subject in fragments. It has been suggested that postmodernist fiction highlights the dispersal of the individual coherent subject and entails destabilised constructions of the feminine.[8] Rhys was suggesting this revision long before, though at the same time paradoxically adhering to precisely those 'feminine' representations which she shows to be fictive.

So, how is Sasha constructed as a subject within the novel? Rhys resists traditional realist systems of character representation, for Sasha is as double-headed and double-faced as the banjo player in the expressionist painting she buys from the Russian Jewish artist in Paris (*GMM*, p.100) and her narrative, though it attempts to preserve a precarious stability and sequence, is insistently fragmented by the operations of memory and fantasy. Indeed in a novel which is full of doublings and distorted reflections[9], the figure in the painting, 'resigned, mocking, a little mad. Standing in the gutter playing his banjo' (*GMM*, p.185) is Sasha's double. Coming back to Paris in late October 1937 on a holiday paid for by a woman friend in London, the middle-aged Sasha tries to maintain her state of numbness and isolation: she finds a furnished room in an 'impasse' and arranges the programme of her days so that there will be 'no gaps'. Yet from the beginning, the project is an illusion; on the very first page she bursts into tears, and the fragile structure of contradictions through which she has constituted her present self is laid bare in her brief life history:

> Saved, rescued, fished-up, half-drowned, out of the deep, dark river, dry clothes, hair shampooed and set. Nobody would know I had ever been in it. Except of course that there always remains something. Yes, there always remains something. (*GMM*, p.10)

Memory leaves its traces which erode boundaries between her present visit and her earlier visits in '1923 or 1924 . . . Was it in 1926 or 1927?' (*GMM*, p.12) and the topography of the city, like Sasha's consciousness, is haunted by ghosts who trail 'in an ordered undulating procession past my eyes. Rooms, streets, streets, rooms . . . ' (*GMM*, p.109).

The deep dark river continues to flow beneath the surface she presents to the world, so that try as she might to mimic the persona of a 'femme convenable', she never quite feels that she is giving a convincing performance:

> Please, please, monsieur et madame, mister, missis and miss, I am trying so hard to be like you. I know I don't succeed, but look how hard I try. (*GMM*, p.106)

Ironically the events of the narrative suggest that she does succeed, for she is mistaken for a rich English woman in a fur coat by two Russians whom she meets in a café and who persuade her to buy the painting of the banjo player, and most significantly she is picked up in the Dome by the gigolo, René. As she reflects with characteristic self-irony:

> Do I really look like a wealthy dame trotting round Montparnasse in the hope of -? After all the trouble I've gone to, is that what I look like? I suppose I do. (*GMM*, p.72)

It is through her relationship with René, which Rhys develops by a complex strategy of doublings, that Sasha rehearses all her subject positions of resistance, refusal and revenge, only to discover that her performance has for once been entirely convincing when René walks out on her. As a divided subject indulging in an anguished series of self-protective gestures, Sasha has invented a deterministic script which results not in the paralysis of feeling for which she had hoped, but in another emotional disaster at the very moment of her painful re-awakening. If, as Abel suggests, René is offering Sasha salvation through sex,[10] then Sasha deliberately prevaricates, retreating from the 'miracle' of emotional contact which she had glimpsed on the dark staircase[11]:

> I have my arms round him and I begin to laugh, because I am so happy. I stand there hugging him, so terribly happy. Now everything is in my arms on this dark landing – love, youth, spring, happiness, everything I though I had lost. I was a fool, wasn't I? to think all that was finished for me. How could it be finished? (*GMM*, p.177)

But such a moment of unity is impossible to sustain, and even as the pair walk into her room the process of fragmentation begins:

> We kiss each other fervently, but already something has gone wrong. I am uneasy, half of myself somewhere else. (*GMM*, p.177)

The desired moment of consummation becomes a 'difficult moment when you are out of practice', to be struggled against and finally deprived of value, 'a game played in the snow for a worthless prize'. The image eloquently focuses Sasha's condition of forlornness and loss.

If Sasha had hoped to evade pain she is not allowed to, for René persists:

> I feel his hard knee between my knees. My mouth hurts, my breasts hurt, because it hurts, when you have been dead, to come alive.
> 'Now everything is going to be all right,' he says.
> ' T'as compris?' he says.
> Of course, the ritual answer is, 'Si, j'ai compris . . .'
> I lie there, thinking 'Yes, I understand.' Thinking 'For the last time'. Thinking nothing. Listening to a high, clear, cold voice. My voice. (*GMM*, p.183)

Not only does she have to suffer the painful restoration of atrophied sexual feeling, but she is forced to undergo the further torments of self-division, where she becomes both participant and voyeuse engaged in a dialogue against herself, listening to a voice which is 'not me speaking.' It is the most painful form of doubled discourse when the feeling subject is silenced and transformed into an object of ironic criticism by another self who speaks out, taunting, suspicious and entirely destructive.[12] Alienated from her own utterance, Sasha loses all power of control over herself or the situation, saying one thing and at the same time silently denying it, putting her arm up over her face to ward off the blows which she expects from René, though it is she who is doing the wounding. When he finally gives up, it is her silent voice which formulates her own need:

> He has moved so quickly that I haven't had time to put my arms

> round him, or to say 'Stay', to say 'Don't do this, don't leave me like this, don't. (*GMM*, pp.184)

But what they both hear as René leaves the room is Sasha's other contemptuous voice:

> Other people's wounds – how funny they are! I shall laugh every time I think about you.' (*GMM*, p.154)

To the end Sasha continues her series of self-lacerating comments, which recognise and deny the affinities between herself and the gigolo, both of them marginalised social figures and in a sense mirror images of each other.

Even when she is left alone, Sasha continues her split scenario, experiencing herself simultaneously occupying two positions as she talks to herself in contradictory voices:

> I cry in the way that hurts right down, that hurts your heart and your stomach. Who is this crying? The same one who laughed on the landing, kissed him and was happy. This is me, this is myself who is crying. The other – how do I know who the other is? She isn't me. Her voice in my head. (*GMM*, p.184)

It is in that tormented inner dialogue that Sasha recognises the banjo player in the picture as her double, and concludes,

> Well, I mustn't sing any more – there you are. Finie la chanson. The song is ended. Finished. (p.185)

The other 'she' is finally silenced by the evidence of the gigolo's generosity. Sasha discovers that he has not taken any of her money, and she pays him the tribute of drinking his health.

The novel ends with Sasha's being very drunk, the state she had wanted to achieve in her room on the Gray's Inn Road and in her room in Paris, when she would not know 'whether it's yesterday, today or tomorrow'. It is then that the procession of jumbled memories and voices come back to haunt her, enacting a savage destruction of romantic fantasy: ' "Madame Vénus se fâchera." "Oh, her!" I say. "What do I care about her?" . . . Venus is dead; Apollo is dead; even Jesus is dead.' Then follows the demented fairground image of the terrible female erotic machine with its innumerable flexible arms, 'At the end of each arm is an eye, the eyelashes stiff with mascara.' (*GMM*, p.186)

Out of this crisis of fragmented subjectivity Sasha emerges, not as a newly unified self but as a self which is emptied out even as it persists in fantasising the gigolo's return:

> Now I am simple and not afraid; now I am myself. He can look at me if he wants to. I'll only say, 'You see, I cried like that because you went away.'
> (Or did I cry like that because I'll never sing again, because the light in my sale cerveau has gone out?) (*GMM*, p.189)

As she lies in her bed, stripped naked, she realises the terrible possibility of the totally decentred self, when as a subject she has ceased to exist. Lying 'as still as if I were dead,' Sasha has at last attained the blankness to which she has for so long aspired. This is her private space emptied of sexual desire as it is of romantic fantasy, where nothingness has been carefully constructed through her explicit recall and rejection of all the traditional discourses about love. Alone and imploring the miracle in which she no longer believes, Sasha approaches the state of self-annihilation at the centre of the whirlpool around which she has been circling:

> Like one of those straws which float round the edge of a whirlpool and is gradually sucked into the centre, the dead centre, where everything is stagnant, everything is calm. (*GMM*, p.44)

This is the end prefigured in her dream of exit near the beginning of the narrative:

> Everywhere there are placards printed in red letters: This Way to the Exhibition, This Way to the Exhibition. But I don't want the way to the exhibition – I want the way out. (*GMM*, p.13)

Underneath all her socially invented personas has run her insistent subtext of refusal:

> And after all, the agitation is only on the surface. Underneath I'm indifferent. Underneath there is always stagnant water calm, indifferent. (*GMM*, p.153)

So Sasha lies in her empty room, waiting for the 'door that will open, the thing that is bound to happen' (*GMM*, p.100). And when the door does open, it is not René (as she knows it will not be), but the thin man in the white dressing gown from the room next door whom she despises and fears. In this final ironic doubling, amid a litany of endings where everything is 'for the last time', Sasha re-enacts the feminine role of seductress as she embraces the wrong man:

> Then I put my arms round him and pull him down on to the bed, saying: 'Yes – yes – yes . . . ' (*GMM*, p.190)

It is a conscious echo of Molly Bloom's eternal female language, but in another version which is the opposite of Molly's *jouissance*, for Sasha has moved far beyond romantic fantasy in even its shabbiest forms. She is approaching her deepest desire, the desire for oblivion.[13] The white robed 'priest' of an 'obscene, half-understood religion' (*GMM*, p.35)(as Sasha had earlier described the man next door) will be making love to a naked corpselike body in Sasha's ultimate gesture of self-abandonment.

Sasha has found a language for articulating the self in process of deconstruction, which is the double-voiced language of parody, a mimicry of other voices in contexts which have been emptied of significance. It is the same strategy that contemporary women writers and feminist theorists have come to adopt in their inscription of female difference.[14] However, for the spaces of non-being, the only language available is the traditional language of metaphor: midnight, the whirlpool, the black hole, the misery of utter darkness, where displacement and deferral characterise Sasha's speaking of her deepest desire; at the dead centre there is only silence.

Sasha's parodic version of Molly Bloom's 'Yes' confirms those elements of complicity and resistance which characterise Rhys's relationship to the canonical works of male modernism. The figure of Molly actually hides two other figures who are unnamed but who lurk behind Sasha. They are *The Waste Land* figures of the typist who also submits to caresses 'which still are unreproved, if undesired,' and behind her the blind gazer Tiresias, who has himself 'foresuffered all / Enacted on this same divan or bed'.[15] Arguably it is part of Rhys's complex strategy of doubling that these shadowy parallels should be there as ghosts in the text, for *Good Morning, Midnight* represents Eliot's urban and spiritual territory from a feminine perspective. Sasha's story takes up many of *The Waste Land* themes – its obsession with history and tradition, urban social conditions, the spiritual and emotional dereliction of a modern city's inhabitants –just as it adopts Eliot's poetic strategies of fragmentation and multivoicedness. More specific still are the intertextual variants on' Death by Water' ('Why didn't you drown yourself,' tho old devil said, 'in the Seine?' *GMM*, p.41), and Sasha's painful narrative which mixes 'memory and desire, stirring /Dull roots with spring rain' ('The Burial of the Dead,'ll.3-4). But the season is not spring, it is autumn; the city is not London but Paris, and Sasha's female anxieties are not the same as those voiced in *The Waste Land*. In Susan Squier's useful formulation, 'Eliot's poem circles around issues of domination and control, and reflects an anxious search for individual autonomy'.[16] Rhys's novel by contrast circles around issues of marginality and resistance, reflecting a sense of heterogeneity within the subject and an anxious search for the dispersal and silencing of the self.

Paris is not a safe place to explore, for its streets are hostile territory for a woman:

> Walking in the night with the dark houses over you, like monsters . . . Then they step forward, the waiting houses, to frown and crush. No hospitable doors, no lit windows, just frowning darkness. Frowning and leering and sneering, the houses, one after another. (*GMM*, p.32)

This is the same perception of female ex-centricity as Marya and Julia registered in Paris, and as Anna felt in London where 'the darkness of the streets has a meaning', though in *Good Morning, Midnight* it is recorded quite explicitly in terms of gender antagonism. It is the social documentation of Paris from a woman's perspective that is the focus of Shari Benstock's brief discussion of *Good Morning, Midnight*, where she fits it together with Djuna Barnes's *Nightwood* (1936) and Anais Nin's *The House of Incest* (1936) as 'the final panel to a triptych of the

Thirties.'[17] However Rhys goes back to 1920s Paris as well, challenging conventional assumptions about the frivolous gaiety of the Jazz Age:

> 'All you young women,' he says, 'dance too much. Mad for pleasure, all the young people . . . Ah, what will happen to this after-war generation? I ask myself. What will happen? Mad for pleasure . . . But we'll take a taxi.' (*GMM*, p.89)

Opposed to this myth is the shock of reality, when the young Sasha tells her escort that she is giddy because she hasn't enough money to eat. He drives off in the taxi leaving her standing on the pavement.

If Sasha has been in her day a flapper figure, so has she also been, appropriately enough, a ghost writer, as she reveals in one of her confessions to René.[18] This rare portrayal of a female writer in a Rhys novel is a significantly self-reflexive gesture, which reveals another facet of Rhys's ambivalent relation to literary tradition and further dimensions of self-irony. For a brief period Sasha was employed as an ammanuensis for a rich woman in Antibes, writing down fairytales which the woman invented, prostituting her talents like René who had also been employed by the same woman. It is inevitable that Sasha should chronicle so amusingly her moment of failure. She recalls that she was accused by the woman of using language which was too simple: 'He thinks it strange that you should write them in words of one syllable' (*GMM*, p.166). That accusation has further dimensions of self-parody for it echoes Rhys's own wry description of *Voyage in the Dark*, 'It's written almost entirely in words of one syllable. Like a kitten mewing perhaps.[19] Here Rhys is speaking back to herself just as Sasha silently speaks back to her employer:

> Persian garden. Long words. Chiaroscuro? Translucent? . . . I bet he'd like cataclysmal action and centrifugal flux, but the point is how can I get them into a Persian garden? . . . Well, I might. Stranger things have happened . . . A blank sheet of paper . . . (*GMM*, p.167)

This passage carries a powerful suggestion of the restricted spaces available to the woman writer, just as it is an ironic comment on her standing in the literary profession that she should be engaged to copy out fairytales while other forms of fiction are not open to her. Sasha remarks on her position as an outsider, linking it explicitly to the gender question when she thinks about a book she will never be able to write:

> 'I'm no use to anybody,' I say. 'I'm just a cérébrale, can't you see that?'
> Thinking how funny a book would be, called 'Just a Cérébrale or You Can't Stop Me from Dreaming.' Only, of course, to be accepted as authentic, to carry any conviction, it would have to be written by a man. What a pity, what a pity! (*GMM*, p.135)

In the male dominated spaces of fiction, as in the city streets, a woman like Sasha has to struggle to retain even a marginal position. Yet Sasha manages to interpellate her feminine version of the failure of love which *The Waste Land* had chronicled in its spelling out of the dynamics of male-female relationships:

> The sea was calm, your heart would have responded
> Gaily, when invited, beating obedient
> To controlling hands. ('What the Thunder Said,' ll.420–2)

As counterpoint to this, Sasha offers her own secular version which blends resistance and antagonism with curious moments that confirm traditional notions of male authority. One of the oddest is her flash of romantic fantasy at the point where she has flatly rejected René's appeal to go back with her to her hotel. As he begins to whistle the march of the Foreign Legion, her inner scenario shifts so that she sees herself in what is presumably the room of a Moroccan house, alone with a man who is also whistling that tune as she anxiously watches for him to turn his head towards her. She is his slave, ill-treated and totally in love with him: 'If he were to die I should kill myself' (*GMM*, p.176). The focus here is on woman's subservience to man, for this is the doomed romance plot about women in love which Rhys repeats with variations in all her novels; it seems there is only one possible structure for male-female relationships and only one female subject position available. What is so strange is that Sasha invents this scene as a private encoding of her desperate need for love and her own condition of beggary, laying out the ambivalent subtext of longing that lies behind her categorical refusal of René's proposition, while acknowledging the dimensions of conscious fabrication in her ironic dismissal of the scene, 'My film-mind . . . ("For God's sake watch out for your film-mind . . . ")' (*GMM*, p.176).[20]

This is Sasha's version of the dark fantasy of female submission which echoes back through the psychic scripts of all Rhys's heroines as she replays the repressed narrative of love, sex and submission grounded in the Mr Howard story. Curiously, as the Black Exercise Book shows, this memory surfaced again while Rhys was writing *Good Morning, Midnight*, 'putting the finishing touches to the wreck' as she called it, when she suddenly remembered Mr Howard's house as she walked along a towpath in England. Significantly, it is at this point that Rhys relates the anguish of writing to the pain of sexual love, for to her they entail a similar condition of enslavement:

> I have given myself up to it this time . . . Not for hope of heaven nor for fear but for love. Was that what I've been always meant to learn?[21]

Such rhetoric is close to that self-surrender which Sasha enacts when she speaks through Molly Bloom's voice. It is an interesting strategy to end a narrative about fragmented female subjectivity and the woman writer's marginality with a male modernist writer's version of a woman speaking. The trajectory of the novel may be traced from the title with its allusion to a female literary tradition to these final words from *Ulysses* with its suggestion of the double voicing of a split subject. (But is it Sasha? Or is it Rhys? Or both?) Rhys is presenting a gendered allegory of the modern condition of unbelonging as her female protagonist's voice, like the voice of the woman writer, is effectively silenced, dispersed within a male-dominated literary space.

# Chapter Six

## *The madwoman comes out of the attic:* Wide Sargasso Sea

I . . . was vexed at her portrait of the 'paper tiger' lunatic, the all wrong creole scenes, and above all by the real cruelty of Mr Rochester.[1]

Jean Rhys's last novel, *Wide Sargasso Sea*, published after a silence of more than twenty-five years[2] is her most rebellious text of all, as if only in old age did she become reckless enough to be explicit about her inward rage, no longer displacing it into stories of female failure in contemporary London and Paris but going straight to the heart of the matter, which was for her the colonial question and the fate of a white Creole woman. This novel displays all the signs of the rebelliousness of a woman's text which Gilbert and Gubar's *The Madwoman in the Attic* was the first to chronicle, but it carries the revolt into a different camp by rebelling against a text by another woman, Charlotte Brontë's 'reactionary nineteenth century romance' *Jane Eyre* (*JRL*, p.157). As Caribbean revisionist history, *Wide Sargasso Sea* challenges Brontë's English assumptions about colonial otherness while situating itself within the same literary conventions of the romance as she had used, so suggesting Rhys's deeply ambivalent relation to English literary and cultural traditions. The novel has been read by recent critics as 'post-colonial counter-discourse' in its challenge to the politics of imperialism.[3] However, it must be added that while such dissent is unquestionably important, this haunting novel escapes the limits of ideological statement. Slipping between reality and dream in spaces that are both textually and historically determined, it manages to elude the ultimate imperialism of definitive interpretation. As a tragic love story it opens out into the territory of romance in a multivoiced telling where the voices that have been eclipsed by the Victorian novel are not only Caribbean ones but also the voice of the Englishman, Mr Rochester. Indeed it is he who offers the most anguished celebration of the wild beautiful Caribbean landscape, and it is through his unspoken monologues as much as through his Creole wife's perspective that the reader glimpses the romantic excess of forbidden desire which is at the heart of this magical text.

Like her other Caribbean novel *Voyage in the Dark, Wide Sargasso Sea* had a long gestatory period. As Rhys put it so startlingly to Francis Wyndham in 1962,

> One thing I have never told you. I wrote this book before! – Different setting – same idea. (It was called 'Le revenant' then). The MSS was lost when I was moving from somewhere to somewhere else and I wonder whether I haven't been trying to get back to what I did. (An impossible effort.) (*JRL*, p.213)

There is some evidence that Rhys had written a version of her *Jane Eyre* novel by 1939 which had been typed up by Leslie Tilden Smith,[4] and she refers occasionally in letters in the 1940s and 50s to her 'novel half done . . . It's about the West Indies about 1780 something' (*JRL*, p.56; p.143). The fascinating question is why she should have returned to this West Indian material at the time she did, between 1957 and 1966. There is the interesting possibility that another West Indian novel, Phyllis Shand Allfrey's *The Orchid House* (1953), may have been an important stimulus for Rhys's creative imagination. Allfrey too was a white Dominican Creole and her narrative contains a neglected plantation house called L'Aromatique and evokes the physical atmosphere of Dominica with its peculiar combination of tropical beauty and unease. Though set in a post-World War I era after Rhys had left Dominica, *The Orchid House* perhaps acted as a necessary catalyst for her imaginative effort of dreaming her way back to the past as she does in her novel.[5]

The writing of *Wide Sargasso Sea* was a laboriously painful process, for it is far more than an imaginative statement about West Indian history; it also contains a strongly felt interpellation of personal loss:

> The West Indies I write of has vanished completely – even the West Indies I knew has vanished. There is not even much record of it. 'West Indies' 'Creole' means something different now. Utterly different.
> They had their own civilisation but it has gone. Even the houses are ruins with few exceptions, even the roads are overgrown. How can I make it seem true?[6]

Rhys conjures up the voices of ghosts in her subtle study of mid-nineteenth century colonial history beneath the layers of personal memory, legend and dream. If we wanted to follow the way suggested but not taken by Spivak of 'loosening the binding of the book,'[7] we could see this as psychic autobiography, with Rhys voicing her own sense of displacement as a white Creole, dispossessed at home and living as an exile in England.

Rhys regarded *Wide Sargasso Sea* as her 'dream book which has often been a nightmare to me' (*JRL*, p.214). Its title apparently came to her in a dream. She told Peggy Kirkaldy, 'I woke up thinking the words "Sargossa Sea" ',[8] though later she said that it was taken from a Creole song (*JRL*, p.253). She only realised that the novel was finished after her dream of childbirth:

> Finally I dreamt that I was looking at the baby in a cradle – such a puny weak thing.
> So the book must be finished, and that must be what I think about it really. I don't dream about it any more. (*JRL*, p.301)

During the writing of the novel, Rhys talked a great deal about her sense of being possessed by an inspirational force outside herself, likening the creative process to 'walking on water' (*JRL*, p.160) and writing to dictation:

> I will finish this book by myself and be passive and write what I am told to write. I don't care any more what happens to it – once written. (*JRL*, p.272)

This passage which prefaces a long discussion about revisions to Parts Two and Three emblematises Rhys's constitutional conflict between attention to the conscious structuring of her writing and the power of her unconscious. Though a version of the novel was typed in August 1963 and Sonia Orwell published Part One of *Wide Sargasso Sea* in the first issue of *Art and Literature* in 1964 (*JRL*, p.254), Rhys was still insisting on revisions and recording clarifications of her story later that year. One of the most significant is in a letter to Francis Wyndham in April that year where she enclosed a poem 'Obeah Night' which she claimed had provided her with the final clue to her novel:

> Only when I wrote this poem – then it clicked – and all was there and always had been. (*JRL*, p.262)

Such activity is typical of Rhys's intuitive methods of working, of getting at the truth of place, character and feeling 'sidelong, sideways' (*JRL*, p.279). It is surely this writing process which produces her curiously anguished mixture of irresponsibility and professionalism:

> This book should have been a dream – not a drama – I know. Still, I want to make the drama *possible*, convincing. (*JRL*, p.216)

The drama of Rhys's novel is the drama of West Indian history focused through the figure of the mad wife in *Jane Eyre*:

> The West Indies *had* a (melo?) dramatic quality. A lot that seems incredible could have happened. And did. Girls *were* married for their dots at that time, taken to England and no more heard of. Houses were burnt down by ex-slaves . . . I don't know if 'obeah' still goes on. But it did. (*JRL*, p.216)

Rhys writes back to Brontë's novel challenging her misrepresentations on thematic and ideological grounds, claiming 'That's only one side – the English side' sort of thing . . . White West Indians . . . have a side and a point of view'. (*JRL*, p.297). She reverses Brontë's text to tell the story from the mad wife's point of view, displacing the centre of interest entirely. It is only the relation between the Creole woman and Rochester matters so that Jane Eyre herself is absent from Rhys's [illegible]. What is marginal becomes central, for 'The Creole is of course the important one. I'm fighting mad to tell her story' (*JRL*, p.157).

No longer is the mad wife a horrid colonial secret to be kept 'locked away, and like all memories a legend. Or a lie',[9] for here Jane Eyre's dark double escapes out of the attic into the fiction. As soon as the speechless raging monster becomes a speaking woman with a history and a logic of her own, she begins to tell a story to which Brontë, with her unquestioning belief in the assumptions of imperialism, was blind. The Creole woman's own version of her marriage effects a complete reversal of Rochester's version which he told to Jane Eyre. Married against her will, deprived by her husband of even her Christian name as well as her fortune and brought into exile, the Antoinette Rochester of Rhys's novel emerges as the victim of a patriarchal plot devised by fathers and sons which chimes with the plot of imperialism. Hers is a story of colonial disablement worked out through a story of the failure of love between a Creole heiress and an Englishman.

The Englishman himself (never named in Rhys's text) presents a different image of the imperialist from Brontë's figure. Whereas in *Jane Eyre* imperialism is understood as England's social mission, with Rochester convinced that he is performing his duty to God and humanity by taking his mad wife back to England, in *Wide Sargasso Sea* his behaviour is exposed as being far less creditable.[10] Instead it shows the male will to dominate combined with a strong impulse toward revenge and punishment. However, the portrait of Rochester is by no means entirely hostile, for the shift to a colonial perspective reveals another side to cross-cultural encounters which is absent from *Jane Eyre*. His visit does make a difference to Rochester, for through the exotic landscape and the girl he marries he catches a glimpse of a territory of romance which lies beyond his grasp. It is the revelation of his desire for that otherness which shocks him into the realisation of his own lack and the limits of imperialism as the standard of absolute value. His relationship with Antoinette charts Rochester's passage beyond 'sanity' into the dangerous realms of desire and dream. Within this romantic dimension erotic and cross-cultural encounters become one and the same, where 'only the magic and the dream are true – the rest's a lie' (*WSS*, p.168). But such disorientation borders on nightmare, and as strangeness becomes estrangement, Rochester resumes the traditional stance of male imperialist authority, denying that experience and silencing the woman's voice which speaks out of that place. Antoinette remains a stranger, eluding him as she had always done. Even in exile she cannot be accommodated or effectively imprisoned, and in the end manages to strike back, taking revenge for all her betrayals.

The 'all wrong creole scenes' are rewritten as Rhys introduces dimensions of Caribbean landscape and culture that Brontë knew nothing about. Instead of a hellish West Indies of 'fiery nights' and hurricanes, Rhys evokes a hauntingly beautiful fallen Paradise, 'a lovely place in any weather, however far I travel I'll never see a lovelier' as Rochester acknowledges (*WSS*, p.164). Rhys's early nineteenth century Jamaica and Dominica create in their historical specificity a distinctive colonial society organised on issues of class and colour which coexists within the political structures of imperialism. The gaps between whites, blacks and coloureds here are as unbridgeable as those between white Creoles and the English, and while Rhys explores a range of white colonial positions from the inside, her view of black and coloured characters remains an external one. As Spivak acutely remarks:

> *Wide Sargasso Sea* marks with uncanny clarity the limits of its own discourse in Christophine, Antoinette's black nurse . . . She cannot be contained in a novel which rewrites a canonical English text . . . in the interest of the white Creole rather than the native.[11]

Hers is one of the unfinished stories, like that of the nameless black boy who is left crying on the road when Rochester leaves Granbois, or of the white Jamaican Creole girl, Louise de Plana, 'Anything might have happened to you, Louise, anything at all, and I wouldn't be surprised' (*WSS*, p.55). Caribbean history is full of disrupted stories and it is through her narrative recording of its gaps and silences as much as through its vanished voices that Rhys replaces the threatening other world on the periphery of Brontë's vision with a community that is 'possible, convincing'.

It is true that *Wide Sargasso Sea* is asserting colonial difference in relation to inherited traditions of Empire, so it is not surprising that the novel is dominated by multiple patterns of determinism. As an historical novel, it is caught within the determinisms of Caribbean social history in the early nineteenth century, just as it is caught within the patterns of British colonial history. Jamaica was one of the oldest British West Indian sugar islands, having been captured from the Spanish in the mid-seventeenth century. However, by the end of the eighteenth and before Rhys's novel opens, it was suffering from economic depression and slave unrest; many of the old plantations had been abandoned or sold to meet debts, and indeed by 1806 the price of Jamaican sugar was less than the cost of its production. By the 1830s when slavery in British colonies was abolished, the plantation economy was already in decline.[12] Set in Jamaica and Dominica in the period immediately after Emancipation in 1838, Rhys's novel inhabits this derelict world as it traces the confusions and ambiguities of the post-slavery era from the perspective of the white Creole class to which Antoinette Cosway's family belonged. She is the inheritor of a fallen Paradise, Coulibri Estate, living with her widowed mother, her idiot brother and a few remaining black servants in a situation which bears witness to the collapse of the plantation system: 'All Coulibri Estate had gone wild like the garden, gone to bush. No more slavery – why should anybody work?' (*WSS*, p.19) It is a fragile world where traditional social codes of interdependency between white and black precariously survive, now emptied of meaning by the legal and economic reversals of Emancipation and continually subject to disruption. Friendship, loyalty and betrayal are bewilderingly entwined, so that a childhood game between white and black can quickly degenerate into a racial confrontation as Antoinette accuses her friend Tia of being a 'cheating nigger' and Tia calls her a 'white cockroach'. Hated by the blacks and despised for their poverty by both blacks and other whites, Antoinette and her mother are the victims of a system the collapse of which has not only dispossessed them as a class but also deprived them as individuals of any means of independent survival.

Her mother's rescue through marriage to the Englishman, Mr Mason, and her alliance with the new colonialism represents the final stages in the destruction of the old way of life.[13] Coulibri Estate is burned down one night by a mob of ex-slaves. Her brother dies, Antoinette is injured in a traumatic confrontation with Tia, and her mother goes mad. There is one moment during the fire which is emblematic of this hybridised colonial culture, as Antoinette recounts an incident as bizarre as any of those Providential interventions in *Jane Eyre*. As Mr Mason prays, 'May God Almighty defend us,' Antoinette adds:

> And God who is indeed mysterious, who had made no sign when they burned Pierre as he slept – not a clap of thunder, not a flash of lightning – mysterious God heard Mr Mason at once and answered him. The yells stopped. (*WSS*, p.42)

But the divine answer to the voice of imperialist Christianity is oddly conflated with the forms of black superstition, for it is the sight of her mother's burning parrot, Coco (the bird that spoke only in French patois), which unnerves the mob:

> It was very unlucky to kill a parrot, or even to see a parrot die. They began to go then, quickly, silently, and those who were left drew aside. (*WSS*, p.43)

Realising the dimension of her loss, Antoinette becomes a displaced person in her own country, entirely dependent on a dowry supplied by her English stepfather and at the mercy of an arranged marriage with an Englishman who has been sent to the West Indies to seek his fortune. So Antoinette is forced to enact another stage in the story of colonial violation, through her individual destiny retracing the lines of dynastic and imperialist history.

It is within that story of exile and madness that *Wide Sargasso Sea* is subject to the determinism imposed by *Jane Eyre*. Writing against it, Rhys can free Antoinette from the stereotype of the Creole lunatic but she cannot actually alter the ending. The *Jane Eyre* story prescribes what happened to Rochester's mad wife: she set fire to Thornfield and killed herself.

Yet there is a third kind of determinism generated within the narrative. Signalled by Antoinette's dreams, this oneiric dimension suggests an alternative pattern of destiny relating directly to the genre of romance, and it is through dream that Rhys's narrative manages to elude and subvert the imperialisms of history and the English literary tradition. Though Antoinette's three dreams occur in the context of cross-cultural encounters with Englishness (Mr Mason's arrival at Coulibri; her stepfather's first mention of Mr Rochester, and the decisive moment of entry into the Brontë text), their psychic dynamic is a sexual one, projecting a female dreamscape of desire and dread. Taking a clue from Rhys's remark to Selma Vaz Dias in 1959, 'All the same my dream must stand for it is the only thing I'm sure of' (*JRL*, p.160), it is possible to trace the correspondence between Antoinette's dreams and Rhys's own adolescent dream recounted in the Mr Howard story in the Black Exercise Book, for Rhys is speaking through fiction out of a private place of repressed memory.[14] It seems to me that these dreams are the strongest witness to the continuities that lie beneath Rhys's fiction, just as they mark her crucial differences from Brontë's imaginative construct. Though Rhys does not question Brontë's analysis of the power relations between the sexes, there is a decisive shift of emphasis here where the dreaming subject is no longer Jane but the Creole wife. In addition Rhys's dreamwork introduces a dimension of erotic sensibility darker and more dangerous than anything that Brontë entertains. It is principally through these dreams with their shadowy reflections and half disclosures that boundaries between the real and the fantastic, history and the present, the self and the other are transgressed, eroding the limits of a story of colonial encounters and opening out into the spaces of Gothic romance.

*Wide Sargasso Sea* belongs more truly to the romance genre than its English predecessor, sharing many of the characteristics of romance outlined by Northrop Frye and Fredric Jameson, with the narrative closely linked to ideas of destiny projected through the animistic forces of black and white magic.[15] This is the only Rhys novel where Caribbean primitive magic is foregrounded in plot. Rhys refers to this language of magic in her letters:

> I realised that he [Rochester] must have fallen for her – and violently too. The black people have or had a good word for it – 'She *magic* with him' or 'he *magic* with her'. Because you see, that is what it is – magic, intoxication. Not 'Love' at all. (*JRL*, p.262)

Though magic relates here to psychology and the dynamics of sexual attraction, it is also linked to Caribbean obeah practices which operate externally to the individual.[16] The powers of black women like Christophine are shown to be dangerous to whites in the obeah seduction scene (which is also the topic of Rhys's poem). It is also a practice forbidden by the white European magic of the law. Obeah territory is on the edge of the novel and yet the scenarios of magical narrative are part of this fictional world. The landscape is transformed into the forest of Antoinette's dreams which becomes in turn the hidden place where Rochester finds himself when he is lost beyond the boundaries of Granbois. This is the space where borders blur and where Jameson's account of the modern fantastic may stand as paraphrase for the effects generated by the dreamlike encounters of the novel:

> The sense of a whole environment slowly gathering, organising itself into a revelation of meaning, or better still, into some new and unimaginable language.[17]

However, the revelation so intimately connected with Caribbean place does not come, and the white protagonists are forced to spend their lives in exile from the dream, where both Antoinette and Rochester recount their stories of failure and betrayal.

Antoinette's is a Gothic story situated in a time-suspended textual space after she has re-entered the *Jane Eyre* story and has had her dream of burning down Thornfield Hall. Though this is not clear till the end of the novel, the title gives the first clue to the suspensions of the narrative. The Sargasso Sea is that becalmed area of the Atlantic Ocean between the West Indies and England, first spotted by Columbus in 1493 and named after the seaweed drifting there, a place of stagnation and suspended animation. Though never named in the novel, it is referred to obliquely by Antoinette in Part Three when she speaks of her passage by sea to England:

> They tell me I'm in England but I don't believe them. We lost our way to England. When? Where? I don't remember, but we lost it. (*WSS*, p.181).

It takes her till the end of the novel to find her way out – not to England, but back to her past into the dream of Coulibri (already destroyed, lost Eden, place of her first betrayal).

The circularity of the novel confounds any sense of a linear arrangement between past and present. (There is no future.) Instead there is a conflation of experiences whch are repeated and distorted in an eddy of connnections and separations, till finally Antoinette's story is swallowed up by the past into another text: *Jane Eyre*. Of course Rhys would choose a Gothic tale like *Jane Eyre* for her revisionist history, for the Gothic is a subversively feminine discourse full of ghosts and innocent female victims, also a vehicle for the covert expression of women's darker feelings of anger and revenge. Gothic celebrates the hidden subversive life which undermines existing social and psychological orders from within (where burning down the house while still inside it is a good example). Arguably the relation between *Jane Eyre* and *Wide Sargasso Sea* is itself a Gothic one, for Rhys as colonial subject is haunted by the imperial text just as the authority of that earlier text is, in turn, threatened by the subversive entry of its post-colonial revision.[18] Gothic is the perfect deviant discourse for repossessing history and telling the story from another angle, that of the victims of history.

The three-part structure of *Wide Sargasso Sea* has interesting implications in a novel which scrutinises the traditional binary oppositions of colonialism and gender. Rejecting the autobiographical quest narrative of *Jane Eyre*, Rhys chooses a characteristically modernist form such as we find in *Nostromo, To the Lighthouse* or *A Passage to India*. Parts One and Three are Antoinette's story told in her own voice, with a gap in the middle dominated by Rochester's voice in Part Two. Though it is tempting to see this as a mirror structure with the first and third parts looking inwards at each other and privileging Antoinette's story, the rift at the centre radically disturbs such a reading. Rochester's story is not only an interruption of Antoinette's, but is itself a partial mirroring of it. This suggests a loss of boundaries between her experience and his, and the consequent need for narrative redefinitions which would reflect the changing positions within cross-cultural encounters. It is only when this impulse towards convergence is denied by

Rochester that the narrative returns to the t
politics of imperialist domination. Part Thre
and a different image of Antoinette, for she
gap of hopelessness, exile and madness to w
reduced. She is the same yet not the same, a
her 'Obeah Night' poem and to which she added a gloss:

> In the poem Mr Rochester (or Raworth) consoles himself or justifies himself by saying that *his* Antoinette runs away after the 'obeah nights' and that the creature who comes back is not the one who ran away. I wish this had been thought of before – for that is part of Obeah . . . No. Antoinette herself comes back but so changed that perhaps she *was* 'lost Antoinette'. I insist that she must be lovely, and certainly she was lost. 'All in the romantic tradition.' (*JRL*, p.263)

Thinking of mirrors and reflections, there is an odd feature about all the mirror images in this novel: it is the separation of the mirror which is operative, not the conjunction of self and image. Antoinette comments on this when, shut in the attic at Thornfield without a mirror, she remembers brushing her hair when she was a girl:

> The girl I saw was myself yet not quite myself. Long ago when I was a child and very lonely I tried to kiss her. But the glass was between us – hard, cold and misted over with my breath. Now they have taken everything away. What am I doing in this place and who am I? (*WSS*, p.180)

Reflections never disclose the self but always a self which is othered or divided in an infinite process of deferral. The traumatic encounter with the black girl, Tia, outside the burning house at Coulibri emblematises Antoinette's impossible desire for self-completion, in what is also a scene of complicity and betrayal:

> When I was close I saw the jagged stone in her hand but I did not see her throw it. I did not feel it either, only something wet, running down my face. I looked at her and I saw her face crumple up as she began to cry. We stared at each other, blood on my face, tears on hers. It was as if I saw myself. Like in a looking-glass. (*WSS*, p.45)

Much later at Thornfield and reduced to the role of

…adwoman, she looks in a mirror but does not recognise herself at all. Instead she sees an image of that negation of self which she has become and from which she flees:

> It was then that I saw her – the ghost. The woman with streaming hair. She was surrounded by a gilt frame but I knew her. I dropped the candle I was carrying and it caught the end of a tablecloth and I saw the flames shoot up . . . There was a wall of fire protecting me. (*WSS*, p.189)

In her dream Antoinette finally discovers the hallucinatory mirror of the past through which she jumps to her death.

Mirrors may function as agents of duplicity within Antoinette's story, but the power of mirrors to reflect and so to make connections is also evident in the mirroring structure of Part Two. If Rochester's story begins and ends by asserting its masculine imperialist differences from Antoinette's colonial text, its substance betrays a shift toward the relativising concept of *différance* when striking similarities between the two positions are revealed. Rochester begins by stating the accomplished facts of his marriage in Jamaica and their arrival at Granbois, Antoinette's 'sweet honeymoon house' on 'one of the Windward Islands' (Rhys's native Dominica). However, that confident male voice is soon invaded by other voices speaking out of black Caribbean culture and history which unsettle his English codes of order. The language he hears is 'not English but the debased French patois they use in this island' (*WSS*, p.67), the colours are 'extreme', the place is menacing and everything is 'too much'. Even the welcome at Granbois disintegrates into giggling and patois, and there are odd loose ends everywhere, like the title of the English book on the shelf in his dressing room, '*Life and Letters of* . . . The rest was eaten away' (*WSS*, p.75). Everything around him signifies that colonial difference which erodes English limits and systems, resulting in Rochester's condition of bewilderment and paranoia. This instability, which is presented as the reality of cross-cultural encounters, has its shadowy parallel not only with Antoinette's later experience in England but with the heroines' states of mind in Rhys's earlier fictions – even to that blankness of mind which had previously seemed an exclusively female condition:

> As for my confused impressions they will never be written. There are blanks in my mind that cannot be filled up. (*WSS*, p.76)

In his relation with Antoinette, Rochester moves out into uncharted territory, as he gives himself over to the place and to his passion for her, when 'My fever weakness left me, so did all misgiving' (*WSS*, p.87). Rochester's secret love story presents an interesting shift from his distanced account of Bertha's sexual excesses in *Jane Eyre*, for in this account he too is implicated in the passion and the violence, initiating Antoinette into sexual experience so that 'very soon she was as eager for what's called loving as I was – more lost and drowned afterwards' (*WSS*, p.92). Their sexual relationship is a violent one as Antoinette submits totally to love, 'dying' for Rochester 'many times. In my way, not in hers,' where pleasure and pain become the same thing, releasing those dark undercurrents which are the hidden subtext of Gothic fiction. As Rochester remarks in an attempt to take his distance:

> It was not a safe game to play in that place. Desire, Hatred, Life, Death came very close in the darkness. Better not know how close. Better not think, even for a moment. Not close. The same. (*WSS*, p.94)

p79.

Such loving opens the way to dangers outside as well as inside, as Rochester soon discovers, for there is always the menace of history. Daniel Cosway's infamous letter arrives filled with its lies and revelations about Antoinette's family and the past, unearthing an old slave history of scandal and racial hatred which threatens the enclosed world of the lovers. Totally bewildered, he stumbles out into the forest:

> I began to walk very quickly, then stopped because the light was different. A green light. I had reached the forest and you cannot mistake the forest. It is hostile. The path was overgrown but it was possible to follow it. (*WSS*, p.104)

It is there that he comes upon more relics of the past – the old French paved road and the ruined stone house – and glimpses the signs of native magic in the bunches of flowers tied with grass under the orange tree. Lost and afraid among 'enemy trees', Rochester cannot know that he has entered the territory of Antoinette's dreams where individuality blurs and where past and future meet. Rochester retraces his steps to that place of disorientation and dread only once more, after the disastrous 'obeah night' though he keeps his visit secret from his wife and everyone else at Granbois.

In this section of the novel, the intermingling of Rochester's voice with the voices of the black servants and the voice of the half-caste Daniel Cosway suggest the degree to which he finds himself caught in the mesh of West Indian cultural history. Not only is he the victim of Antoinette's disastrous love potion but he is also the avenger of his own outraged male sexuality, enacting continuities between the old and the new colonialism as he seduces Amélie in the room next to his wife's:

> You abused the planters and made up stories about them but you do the same thing. You send the girl away quicker and with no money or less money, and that's all the difference. (*WSS*, p.146)

In what is to be her final outburst, Antoinette speaks her female and colonial resentment against imperialism and its hypocrisies, refuting Rochester's concept of justice as 'a damn cold lie' which has destroyed her as surely as it destroyed her mother before her.

That confrontation spells the impossibility of any convergence between Antoinette and Rochester, for they speak across unbridgeable gaps of mutual misunderstanding, suspicion and betrayal. It is on this occasion that Rochester calls his wife 'Bertha' for the first time, and it is against her will:

> Bertha is not my name. You are trying to make me into someone else, calling me by another name. I know, that's obeah too. (*WSS*, p.147)

Rochester does seem to be engaging in a kind of intertextual obeah here by summoning up the name of Brontë's mad wife, and the significance of this is underlined as Antoinette begins to show signs of violent behaviour from this point on:

> She smashed another bottle against the wall and stood with the

> broken glass in her hand and murder in her eyes. 'Just you touch me once. You'll soon see if I'm a dam' coward like you are.' (*WSS*, p.149)

Biting and cursing, she becomes the mad Bertha Mason of *Jane Eyre*, 'this red-eyed wild-haired stranger who was my wife shouting obscenities at me' (*WSS*, p.149).

However, the overlap with *Jane Eyre* is not yet complete, for Rochester has to have his last confrontation with otherness in the person of Christophine, whose 'dark voice coming from the darkness' forces him into an echo chamber where he sees another image of himself, not as English gentleman but as violator and thief:

> She is Creole girl and she have the sun in her. Tell the truth now. She don't come to your house in this place England . . . No, it's you come all the long way to her house – it's you who beg her to marry. And she love you and she give you all she have. Now you say you don't love her and you break her up. What you do with her money, eh? (*WSS*, p.158)

Rochester cannot tolerate Christophine's view which challenges those assumptions on which his own superiority is based. In opposition to her black magic he invokes the white magic of the law against her, and Christophine walks out of the novel.[19]

Having expelled Christophine, Rochester resumes his imperialist stance with a vengeance, subduing Antoinette in a silent confrontation of wills:

> I did it too. I saw the hate go out of her eyes. I forced it out. And with the hate her beauty. She was only a ghost. A ghost in the grey daylight. Nothing left but hopelessness. *Say die and I will die. Say die and watch me die.* (*WSS*, p.170)

All that is left is the tormenting echo of their love talk as he forges her into his image of a mad woman, so that she becomes the doll-like object of his litany, '*Marionette, Antoinette, Marionetta, Antoinetta*' (*WSS*, p.154). In their farewell to Granbois Antoinette has been forced into the position of the colonial other in her own place, where blankness and silence are all that is allowed:

> 'What right have you to make promises in my name? Or to speak for me at all?'
> 'No, I had no right, I am sorry. I don't understand you.
> I know nothing about you, and I cannot speak for you.' (*WSS*, p.171)

Emptied of 'mad conflicting emotions', Rochester is 'sane' and 'in control' again as he sets out for England with his mad Creole wife. Nevertheless he is forced to recognise the limits of his power, and this knowledge spells his own irretrievable sense of loss:

> Above all I hated her. For she belonged to the magic and the loveliness. She had left me thirsty and all my life would be thirst and longing for what I had lost before I found it. (*WSS*, p.172)

Part Two ends, not with this statement of romantic longing, but with the word 'nothing.' As Antoinette is left with nothing, so is Rochester. They are both hollowed out by their encounter, and their tragedy is emblematised in Rochester's comment on the Caliban figure of the nameless boy whose loss is beyond Rochester's comprehension:

> 'Who would have thought that any boy would cry like that. For nothing. Nothing . . . (*WSS*, p.173)

In Part Three Antoinette resumes her story at Thornfield Hall within the enclosed spaces of Brontë's text, imprisoned inside the Victorian stereotype of the mad Creole wife. Yet, by allowing Antoinette to tell her own story, Rhys might be seen to be playing games with Brontë's representation of female madness, reversing the image to reveal its limits as surely as she exposed the limits of Brontë's imperialist assumptions. It is a strategy neatly formulated by Luce Irigaray in her discussion of hysteria as a form of female performance:

> To play with mimesis is thus, for a woman, to try to recover the place of her exploitation by discourse, without allowing herself simply to be reduced to it.[20]

Antoinette is still a destructive and disorderly presence, but when seen from the inside her behaviour is no longer reducible to the irrationality of self-estrangement. Instead, it becomes the mask for her private act of painful recuperation as she struggles to restore that old relation between her image and herself which has been destroyed by Rochester:

> Names matter, like when he wouldn't call me Antoinette, and I saw Antoinette drifting out of the window with her scents, her pretty clothes and her looking-glass. (*WSS*, p.180)

In the absence of a mirror, she has to retrieve her past self from fragments of memory and from shreds of evidence like her old red dress whose meaning she cannot quite decipher. Insistently probing her own question, 'What am I doing in this place and who am I?' (*WSS*, p.180) she finds her answer through the continuities of dream:' Now at last I know why I was brought here and what I have to do. (*WSS*, p.190)

Part Three does look back and reflect Part One as Antoinette finds her way home through dreams to Coulibri.The fire at the end is and is not the fire at the beginning, for this mirror image is also a duplicitous one. The present is quite literally consumed by the past and Antoinette's moment of authenticity is also the moment of her destruction. As she enters her dream for the last time she steps out not into the forest but into the house, and now she is alone as she comes out of the attic. She is the ghost woman 'whom they say haunts this place' and whom she hopes to avoid. The rooms of Thornfield dissolve into the rooms of her childhood in a kind of double exposure so that she sees 'the tree outside and the shadows of the leaves on the floor, but I saw the wax candles too and I hated them. So I knocked them all down.' (*WSS*, p.154) As the fire begins she sees the ghost in the mirror, but she runs away from her with the fire speading out behind her. Pausing out on the battlements,' I turned round and saw the sky. It was red and all my life was in it (*WSS*, p.189).

As Coulibri is recreated by her imagination, so Antoinette jumps into that dream of yearning in order to find herself by rejoining Tia, her own dark double:

> But when I looked over the edge I saw the pool at Coulibri. Tia was there. She beckoned to me and when I hesitated, she laughed. I heard her say, You frightened? And I heard the man's voice, Bertha! Bertha! All this I saw and heard in a fraction of second. And the sky

> so red. Someone screamed and I thought, *Why did I scream?* I called 'Tia!' and jumped and woke. (*WSS*, p.189)

Even in the dream there is a radical disjunction signalled in Tia's mocking laugh: her double is still beyond her, but Antoinette wakes up before that betrayal is re-enacted. The whole dream is haunted by its own doubleness, for it is both celebration of and elegy for a past which cannot be regained though it may be glimpsed at its moment of dissolution.

The dream functions as a kind of modernist epiphany, which might be compared with Yeats's celebration of the Gore Booth's Georgian mansion Lissadell:

> Arise and bid me strike a match
> And strike another till time catch:
> Should the conflagration climb,
> Run till all the sages know.
> We the great gazebo built,
> They convicted us of guilt;
> Bid me strike a match and blow.[21]

However, the moment of epiphany in *Wide Sargasso Sea* is endlessly deferred, for Antoinette only dreams her act of reconciliation and revenge. She wakes up and is about to set fire to Thornfield as she walks along the 'dark passage'; then the novel ends. Her going along that passage is also her journey back into another text, *Jane Eyre*, which is the only place where her story can have its ending. Antoinette is indeed becalmed, a ghost out of another novel. Yet she can still challenge the limits and the blindness of imperialism, for her story makes it impossible ever to read *Jane Eyre* in the same way again now that the gaps in Brontë's text have been exposed.

Jane Eyre once asked two searching questions of nobody in particular:

> What crime was this, that lived incarnate in this sequestered mansion, and could neither be expelled nor subdued by the owner? – What mystery, that broke out, now in fire and now in blood, at the deadest hour of night?[22]

Rhys vouchsafes Jane an answer without ever acknowledging her existence. The answer actually stretches across her two

Caribbean novels, *Voyage in the Dark* and *Wide Sargasso Sea*, the mystery being signed with blood in one and with fire in the other. It is the mystery of a female colonial sensibility offering its own critique of patriarchy and of imperialism by flooding over or burning up traditional structures of containment, even at the cost of its own annihilation. Moreover, that crime which can neither be expelled nor subdued implicates the owner of the sequestered English mansion as well as his prisoner. Here Rhys writes in the threat of otherness which always exists not on the periphery but deep within the master narratives themselves, enacting that secret drama of *différance* where 'Desire, Hatred, Life, Death came very close in the darkness . . . Not close. The same'(*WSS*, p.94)

# Chapter Seven

# *'There is no penny and no slot': Jean Rhys's Late Stories*

If I live I will call my next and last book *There is no penny and no slot* and if you pinch that title or variations I'll climb up to your window and give you nightmares. (This is a joke.)

(Letter to Selma Vaz Dias, 30 August, 1963)[1]

It seems fitting that as Rhys did not call her last book 'There is no penny and no slot' my last chapter dealing with her late stories should dare to adopt her title and the deconstructive perspective it implies. These stories individually and collectively refute traditional ideas of order as falsifications (her own word is 'lies'), insisting instead on the unaccommodated remainders which will never fit into any system and which by their very existence call any system into question. It is the same dissident narrative voice which told those 'other stories' in her first collection back in the 1920s. However, there is a shift of emphasis here, for many of the stories in Rhys's last two collections adopt a decentred perspective as they dismantle the cultural fictions which persuade 'everybody' to believe in 'the non existent penny and the invisible slot' (*JRL*, p.239). None of these stories is about women in love for that old centring fantasy has been dispersed; instead, they are about figures (mainly women) who are isolated and alone, though again they are the dissident voices which challenge the grand narratives of patriarchy and imperialism.

Taking my cue from Rhys, I do not propose to treat either *Tigers are Better-Looking* or *Sleep It Off Lady* as a whole, for these collections themselves were assemblages put together from across the range of Rhys's published and unpublished work over many years.[2] *Tigers are Better-Looking* was made up from a collection that was ready for publication in 1945 (*JRL*, p.40), though when it appeared in 1968 there were alterations and an interesting echo from the 1920s in a selection of nine stories (and an extract from Ford's Preface) from *The Left Bank. Sleep It Off Lady* was even more of a miscellany, containing some stories written in the 1920s and some published as recently as 1975. As Rhys wrote to her agent Olwen Hughes:

> I've discovered some stories I thought I'd lost – some that I wrote in Paris and one free translation. Not good enough. There is one called 'The Insect World' which might do – about this last war – but it's rather long and I've lost the first page which was important and I can't remember it.[3]

This last collection was finished with the help of Gini Stevens from Deutsch, for Rhys was by then so infirm that she could work only for short periods and by dictation. It was Ms Stevens who typed and retyped successive versions in order to get the stories into the form in which Rhys would agree to publish them. In June 1975 she wrote to her old friend Oliver Stoner:

> The stories are finished – after a fashion. You can't imagine my relief. Also a lost feeling.[4]

I shall discuss five stories from these two collections, and two others which resisted even that accommodation. (One of them, 'I Spy a Stranger', Rhys's editor, Diana Athill, rejected as 'too bitter to be included'). My choice of stories and order of arrangement are designed to illustrate significant Rhys positions in relation to gender, colonialism and modernism, the three elements through which, as I have argued, her writing was determined. In two of the stories I quote extensively from early drafts in the Jean Rhys collection in the McFarlin Library in order to trace details of Rhys's writing processes and to show the significance of her successive revisions where the transformations of writing reshape autobiographical record into fictional artefact.[5] Many of these stories interweave sexual politics with the politics of colonialism, while several of her

London stories make connections between a modernist urban poetics and the alienated female condition. Rhys presents figures and states of feeling that resist classification as she ranges through a dazzling variety of short story forms that include fragmented multivoiced narratives and some that imitate the classic modernist structures of epiphany, only to resolve themselves in moments of dislocation and loss. Indeed, several may be described as structures of disarrangement, where disrupted narrative becomes the means of subverting traditional concepts of order and authority.[6]

'Let Them Call It Jazz,'[7] Rhys's Holloway Prison story told in the voice of a black West Indian woman in London, links gender and colonial politics to the urban environment through its female counter-discourse which is always discredited and finally silenced.[8] Another London story, 'Tigers are Better-Looking,'[9] told this time from a disaffected male perspective, again links gender politics to feminised urban poetics, where a Bloomsbury journalist experiences London from an alienated female perspective. But the carnivalesque nightmare vision is brief; failure is rejected as a feminine flaw, and by the end the traditional rhythms of the system are re-established. In contrast to this multivoiced male ventriloquist act is 'The Sound of the River,'[10] a story about a woman's silence which is swallowed up in the deafening subtext of her confrontation with death. I include two Caribbean childhood stories, 'Goodbye Marcus, Goodbye Rose,'[11] which represents the late resurfacing of Rhys's traumatic adolescent sexual encounter with Mr Howard, and 'The Day they Burned the Books'[12] where a different aspect of colonial encounters is figured in the confrontation of mutual hostility between whites and blacks. This story demonstrates the deeply problematic colonial relation with European traditions, but whereas that story flashes out into a final elusive epiphany, 'Temps Perdi', another Caribbean story,[13] resists any moment of resolution at all. Instead, through a series of seemingly unconnected anecdotes, the narrative presents a devastating historical analysis of power politics from the point of view of colonial and female victims.The World War II story 'I Spy a Stranger'[14] demonstrates the same brutal process of 'othering' conducted in England itself, where explicit connections are made between male misogyny and the war mentality. The woman who engages in the sexual battle on the domestic front is silenced by the very procedures which were instituted to suppress dissidents who threatened national security; she ends up as another mad woman in an attic. No wonder one of Rhys's last stories was called 'Who Knows What's Up in the Attic?' Her female narrator's answer is significant for what it leaves out: 'Not I for one. I wouldn't dare look,'[15] though of course Rhys does look at the female figures like Antoinette and Laura who have been shut up there.

## *'Let Them Call It Jazz'*

After her brief Holloway Prison experience, Rhys wrote to Peggy Kirkaldy:

> Dreadful Holloway. They have a song there that haunts me, the gals I mean, in fact the whole place haunts me, but what can I do? I feel I ought to write but nobody would publish the stuff.[16]

Nevertheless Rhys did write about it in 1960 in what she called 'stylised patois'. Selina Davis's story is presented as emblematic of the immigrant woman's position in urban culture where every effort is made to marginalise and silence her. In a London which is inhospitable, dishonest and unjust, Selina is robbed of her money, persecuted for her failure to conform to English social convention, and locked up in Holloway for being 'drunk and disorderly' and 'causing a disturbance'. However, instead of prison breaking her, it constitutes Selina's salvation for it is there that she hears an anonymous woman singing from the punishment cells: 'She tell the girls cheerio and never say die' (*TABL,* p. 64).This song is the miracle which gives Selina new hope. From that point on, she resumes power over her own life; refusing to be a victim she becomes a survivor instead.[17]

Told from Selina's point of view, this is a strong statement of female defiance against English racial prejudice and social exclusion, though the gender politics are by no means simple. When Selina says, 'Don't talk to me about London. Plenty people there have heart like stone' (*TABL,* p.47), the most flinty-hearted in her experience are not the men but the women – landladies, neighbours and prison officers. Yet it is a woman's song which saves her and it is through her friendship with another coloured girl that she manages to find her niche in London society. If it is a man who offers her shelter, it is also a man who steals her Holloway song from her. It would seem that gender politics are more intricately registered in this story than racial politics, which work on a much simpler pattern of binary opposition, from the Notting Hill landlady's accusation, 'These people terrible liars' (*TABL*, p.53) to the woman next door's remark, 'At least the other tarts that crook installed here were *white* girls' (*TABL*, p.57). It is against English hostility to racial and cultural difference that Selina struggles to make her lyric protest.

The story is pervaded by the sound of women's singing – first of all, Selina's songs in the suburban garden in south London which are so unacceptable to her neighbours, and then the Holloway song which is at the centre of the story. These songs constitute a code of female resistance to authority, as Selina's songs of defiance echo her grandmother's Caribbean patois songs and as the Holloway song bears witness to the women prisoners' solidarity. Singing challenges the imposition of limits, and it is this celebration of excess that the system strives to silence. It is when Selina goes outside into the garden singing and dancing barefoot that her confrontation with the neighbours occurs: goaded by their whispered taunts, she throws a stone through their stained glass window. From their point of view her behaviour is socially unacceptable and to be suppressed by law, but Selina sees it from a different perspective:

> Sometime I think, 'I'm here because I wanted to sing' and I have to laugh. (*TABL*, p.63).

But if it is a song which has got her into prison, it is also a song which saves her:

> It's a smoky kind of voice, and a bit rough sometimes, as if those old dark wall theyselves are complaining, because they see too much misery – too much. But it don't fall and die in the courtyard; seems to me it could jump the gates of the jail easy and travel far, and

> nobody could stop it. I don't hear the words – only the music. (*TABL*, p.64)

This is Selina's miracle of deliverance, as her language with its Biblical overtones suggests:

> One day I hear that song on trumpets and these wall will fall and rest . . . I know now that anything can happen, and I don't want to stay lock up here and miss it (*TABL*, p.64)

Having come to life again, she manages to invent an acceptable persona for herself by learning English social codes, adding as a damning indictment of the system that she has learned to lie, and that is the reason why she survives in London. But this survival is at a price, for Selina is silenced ('I never sing now,' *TABL*, p.67) and finally she is robbed of her last possession. Her precious Holloway song is taken from her by a man who hears her whistling it at a party; he jazzes it up and sells it, then sends her five pounds with thanks, as she was 'quite a help'. The story ends with Selina's see-saw of emotions under this assault, as she contemplates her loss. Selina no longer cries out in protest at injustice; instead, she shrugs eloquently, which is her silent triumph over misunderstanding and also her recognition of social realities:

> Even if they played it on trumpets . . . no walls would fall so soon. 'So let them call it jazz,' I think, and let them play it wrong. That won't make no difference to the song I heard.
> I buy myself a dusty pink dress with the money. (*TABL*, p.67)

## *'Tigers are Better-Looking'*

In contrast to this colonial woman's story with its measure of acquiescence and indifference, the very title of Rhys's other London story, 'Tigers are Better-Looking' with its 'streak of disaster-defying humour'[18] highlights a savage criticism of the predatory masculine social ethic of the modern city. This nightmare carnivalesque version of London is refracted through a male narrating consciousness, when Mr Severn, a Bloomsbury journalist, suddenly finds himself suffering from a shift in vision which allows him for a brief time to share the perspective of those others in London who have to survive outside the protection of the social system. The narrative is structured around the two kinds of carnival in which he participates: on the one hand, the prescribed social festivity of King George V and Queen Mary's Silver Jubilee in May 1935, and on the other, the subversive London night-time carnival whose promiscuity and fragmented exchanges offer an alternative vision of social reality.

This multivoiced narrative begins with a splitting open of the norms of social discourse in the letter of rejection that Mr Severn receives from his lover Hans: ' "Mein Leib, Mon Cher, My Dear, Amigo," the letter began' (*TABL*, p.68). With its polyglot opening and dire criticisms of pretentious London society, the letter goes on to its memorable accusation against the meanness and ferocity of Mr Severn's countrymen:

> I got the feeling that I was surrounded by a pack of timid tigers waiting to spring the moment anybody is in trouble or hasn't any money. *But tigers are better-looking, aren't they?* (*TABL*, p.68)

However, it is the final term of abuse that collapses Mr Severn's facade, for Hans's most vicious blow is to call him a 'tame grey mare', and Mr Severn finds himself suddenly cast into the feminine and as a result adopting a cross-gendered view of London. Instead of writing his weekly column for the Australian newspaper and projecting the imperial voice to the colonies in his account of the Jubilee celebrations, he finds himself adopting a sceptical viewpoint, dismantling the fictions of royalty and empire,seeing the King and Queen as 'victims bowing to victimised' and as 'bloodless sacrifices', rephrasing 'The Sun Never Sets on the Empire' as 'somewhere the sun is shining, even if it doesn't shine on everybody' (*TABL*, p.69). To see from the tame grey mare's point of view is to be disabled from writing at all.

Hoping to find relief from his feeling of rejection and professional failure, Mr Severn first goes to the pub, then embarks on his 'Nighttown' experience with two female companions, wandering from Shaftesbury Avenue to Soho through Rhys's peculiarly depressing nightclubs with their high prices and bad music.[19] It is here that Mr Severn's drunken and distorted vision refracts Hans's accusations through his own experiences of the grotesque and the absurd. First he draws caricatures on the tablecloth which reduce human faces to bestiality:

> *Pictures, pictures, pictures . . . Faces, faces, faces . . . Like hyaenas, like swine, like goats, like apes, like parrots. But not tigers, because tigers are better-looking, aren't they?* (*TABL*, p.74)

When he is thrown out of the club, he gets into a fight, shouting, 'Tally-ho! What price the tame grey mare?' (*TABL*, p.76) He then finds himself, together with one of his companions, an Irishwoman named Maidie Richards, in prison for the night on charges of being drunk and disorderly.

For the first time Mr Severn is forced to contemplate his kinship with those helpless others who scribble on prison walls their garbled messages of defiance, love and hopelessness, and as he lies down with his face to the wall, he sees 'on a level with his eyes, the words "I died waiting." ' (*TABL*, p.78). He has a sudden glimpse of what living in London might mean for a woman like Maidie Richards as her word 'adapted' suddenly swings into focus, 'Adapted to the livid sky, the ugly houses, the grinning policemen, the placards in shop windows' (*TABL*, p.81).This is the prelude to Mr Severn's moment of epiphany, a moment so devastating that he retreats from it in shock as he does from the woman who has made him see it. For Maidie Richards goes too far when she identifies herself and Mr Severn as doubles. Her image of the ageing woman bears a resemblance to the 'tame grey mare' which is too close for confort, and Mr Severn recoils from her as his male mechanism of recovery springs into action: '"*Good*-bye," said Mr Severn, giving her a black look and ignoring her outstretched hand. "We" indeed!' (*TABL*, p.81)

After a break , the last part of the story presents a London daytime vision of normalcy as Mr Severn walks back to his flat, counting his steps along Coptic Street. Incongruities shift back into harmony and his vision is 'reframed' as he contemplates the street from his window. In a last eruption of the carnivalesque spirit an old gentleman carrying a walking stick suddenly tranforms himself into a street clown, 'balancing the stick on the end of his nose, walked backwards and forwards, looking up expectantly' (*TABL*, p.82). But faced with the blankness of the houses, he is forced back into a pose of respectability and 'vanished round the corner.' Just as the old street performer vanishes, so does the Joycean cacophony:

> 'Who pays? Will you pay now, please? You don't mind if I leave you, dear? I died waiting. (Or was it I died hating?) That was my father speaking. Pictures, pictures, pictures. You've got to be young. But tigers are better-looking, aren't they? SOS,SOS,SOS . . . You've got to be younger than we are . . . ' Other phrases, sauve and slick, took their place. (*TABL*, p.82)

The rhythms of convention close over Mr Severn's jagged insights. The story ends with the confident sound of his typewriter tapping out the word 'JUBILEE', though the narrative itself has unleashed a host of contradictory voices within London society in the mid 1930s which threaten to undo 'penny in the slot' responses and which challenge the 'swing' of legitimised social discourse.[20]

## *'The Sound of the River'*

'The Sound of the River' is another story about transgressing borderlines, but this time the boundaries are drawn between human and non-human, life and death. This is the story of a woman's fears and forebodings which find their affirmation in the sudden dreadful knowledge that the man in bed beside her is dead. As the distillation of a subjective state, the narrative presses beyond the limits of language, resorting to a figurative texture of natural imagery as it maintains a delicate balance on the edge of otherness.

The story has its autobiographical basis in Rhys's response to the death of her second husband Leslie Tilden Smith from a heart attack on 2 October 1945, and the 'first draft' exists in the form of a letter which Rhys wrote to his daughter Mrs Phyllis Smyser a week later telling her about her father's death.[21] This letter is important for its statement of personal grief and as a model of what Rhys elides and condenses in the process of transforming fact into fiction. Interestingly, this account tells a different version of events: it is as if the story filters out details, telescoping the woman's feelings around the death and leaving her much more isolated and unprotected than Rhys actually was at the time. Prefacing her account with the words, 'I'll try to tell you exactly what happened,' Rhys goes on to tell Phyllis Smyser that they were staying in an isolated cottage on Dartmoor when one morning her husband complained about a terrible pain in his chest. Rhys went out to telephone for a doctor, but without success. When she returned she heard a strange groaning noise and discovered that her husband was unconscious. Running back to the phone, she managed to call a doctor and then returned to the cottage in time to take his hand in hers as he died. In a slightly different version which she wrote to Peggy Kirkaldy, she said, 'He died really while I was trying to telephone for help from the nearest house, so we didn't even say goodbye.'[22] She was able to get help from three people passing by, who waited with her till the doctor arrived; they also contacted her brother Colonel Rees Williams who came to assist her with funeral arrangements the next day. Rhys refers to her 'dreadful forebodings' during the preceding few months but adds, 'Dreams and forebodings are vague things. No one will take them seriously.'

It is around this loneliness and fear that Rhys's story coalesces, as she refigures the time preceding the man's death and the event itself. Focalised almost entirely through the woman's consciousness of metaphysical dread, the third person narrative uses a technique similar to Expressionist representations of psychic or 'soul states', whereby images function as agents of connection between intuitive perceptions and elemental forces.[23] However, Rhys proceeds differently from the dehumanising distortions of much Expressionist writing, keeping always the sense of individual responsiveness, though defamiliarising domestic scenarios in disturbing ways. The story begins with a man and woman lying in bed talking, but this comfortable familiarity is undercut by their conversation. They are talking about fear:

> 'But what are you afraid of? How do you mean afraid?'
> She said, 'I mean afraid like when you want to swallow and you can't.'

> 'All the time?'
> 'Nearly all the time.'
> 'My dear, really. You are an idiot.'
> 'Yes, I know.'
> Not about this, she thought, not about this. (*TABL*, p.138)

With its registration of gaps and failures in communication, the narrative assumes the form of an interior monologue with brief surfacings into conversation.[24] Most of the time it is an imagistic vehicle for the female subject's state of fear and dread which cannot be named, for 'there aren't any words for this fear. The words haven't been invented' (*TABL*, p.139). It would seem that the focus of fear is the river outside, but the man and the woman perceive it differently. Is it 'very silent' (as she thinks) or does it 'make a row' (as he thinks)? Does it look 'frozen' or is it 'very much alive in an uncanny way'? This instability is a source of terror to the woman, but her fear is all pervasive as it spills over into the non-human world, touching her like a furry otter, trying to get in like the yellow bird beating its wings against the window:

> 'Oh what a pretty bird.' Fear is yellow. You're yellow. She's got a broad streak of yellow. They're quite right, fear is yellow. 'Isn't it pretty? And isn't it persistent? It's determined to get in . . . ' (*TABL*, p.141)

As the woman lies beside the sleeping man, wishing he would stay awake to comfort her, there is no comfort as words slip sideways in the dark: 'Go on. Pull yourself together, pull yourself to pieces'. (*TABL*, p.142) Thinking 'it'll be fine tomorrow', she at last falls asleep.

Without transition the next sentence reads, 'I knew it would be fine today.' With sunlight comes an absence of fear and only the memory of a dream of trees groaning and wind in telegraph wires. The woman chatters on to the silent man beside her, and then comes the dawning of knowledge which her subconscious mind had deflected, as she touches his hand. Suddenly the fear is inside her, focused through the image of her own heart:

> It swelled and grew jagged claws and the claws clutched her driving in deep. 'Oh God, 'she said and got up and drew the curtains and saw his face in the sun.'Oh God,' she said staring at his face in the

> sun and knelt by the bed with his hand in her two hands not speaking not thinking any longer. (*TABL*, pp.142–3)

A gap in the text signals a switch to the conversation between the woman and the doctor about her husband's death, where her responses are vague and uncertain. 'I thought it was a dream,' 'I don't know,' 'I didn't know what to do.' Yet her silence at the end hides a very different apprehension, which is her overwhelming certainty of death:

> She thought, Yes, of course I knew. I was late because I had to stay there listening. I heard it then. It got louder and closer and it was in the room with me. I heard the sound of the river.
> I heard the sound of the river. (*TABL*, p.144)

This terrible moment of epiphany may be read as Rhys's secular version of Psalm LXIX. It brings her curiously close to Jane Eyre's experience of desolation:

> 'The waters came unto my soul; I sank in deep mire; I felt no standing; I came into deep waters; the floods overflowed me.[25]

A final point might be made about the politics of gender encoded in this story. Though her husband affectionately refers to her fears as idiotic, and the doctor is condescending and suspicious, there is no available language through which the woman might express her apprehensions directly. It is against that sense of negation and helplessness that she tells her story, finding through natural images an objective correlative for her feelings where events themselves silently confirm her intuitive knowledge.

## *'Goodbye Marcus, Goodbye Rose'*

'Goodbye Marcus, Goodbye Rose' is again a fictional transformation of autobiographical experience for which the documentary evidence is available, for this is the final version of the Mr Howard story recorded in the Black Exercise Book. (See Chapter 1.) Several drafts chronicle the emergence of this late story, which seems to function as a structure of containment, drained of the pains of the original narrative and without a hint of the ravelled threads that continued to trail through Rhys's own life from her encounter with Mr Howard.[26]

Set in Dominica, it is presented as a girl's growing-up story, told in the third person as the narrative of the twelve-year-old Phoebe who recounts her fascination with the handsome old Englishman, Captain Cardew, and the details of her mental seduction. The story begins with the captain's song, and it is his voice that dominates their relationship, for Phoebe herself is an almost silent listener throughout. This promises to be another colonial encounter with Englishness, dramatised within a male–female relationship, where again (as with Antoinette and Rochester) language functions as the instrument of domination. Indeed, this is exactly what happens as the elderly man spins his 'ceaseless talk of love' to the girl, though the process is infinitely more delicate and bewildering to Phoebe than the formulaic colonial–gender grid of domination and seduction would suggest.

Their encounter is situated within rigid codes of social decorum which predetermine the captain's position of authority as a family friend and Phoebe's position of submission and compliance as a 'little girl' privileged to receive the captain's gallant attentions. Like her island she is 'attractive and unspoilt', playing at the game of being 'a grown-up girl' and totally unprepared to act in her own defence. One day sitting on a bench in the Botanical Gardens and talking about 'a place in England called the Kew', suddenly the captain asks her age and makes an astonishing gesture:

> His hand, which had been lying quietly by his side, darted towards her, dived inside her blouse and clamped itself around one very small breast. (*SIOL*, p.26)

Under this assault, the girl's instinct is to freeze like a wild animal, while the captain keeps his hand there until another couple come along, at which point he calmly removes it. In a story about the power of language, this initial silent act of physical violation is peculiarly significant, not least because of Phoebe's equally astonishing response: 'As they walked she looked up at him as though at some aged but ageless god' (*SIOL*, p.27). She does not question his authority nor does she blame him for his incomprehensible behaviour in the glance which combines her childish admiration with a new inarticulate sexual awareness.

The narrative continues as a registration of transgression where the girl, powerless to act against the codes of good manners imposed by the adult-child relationship, becomes the captain's victim, a silent listener as he tells his peculiar serial stories about love:

> He'd explain that love was not kind and gentle, as she had imagined, but violent. Violence, even cruelty, was an essential part of it. He would expand on this, it seemed to be his favourite subject. (*SIOL*, p.28)

Shocked and fascinated, doubting and resistant, Phoebe does not share his sexual fantasy; Cardew's stories are inflicted on her mind as his hand had once been inflicted on her body and because of her vulnerability they are inflicted on her imagination. In the end, though innocent, Phoebe is blamed as his accomplice - accused by his wife as a 'really dreadful little liar' and regarded with suspicion by her mother. It is really the women's responses rather than Cardew's stories themselves which convince Phoebe of her own sinfulness, offering a curious (but characteristically Rhysian) exoneration of the man here, as well as an assertion of Phoebe's innocence. The relationship ends only when Cardew's wife insists that they go back to England, and it is in the context of codes of polite behaviour (of formal goodbyes and shaking hands) that Phoebe sees him for the last time, 'not quite realizing that she was very unlikely ever to see him again' (*SIOL*, p.29).

The ending signals a different positioning of Phoebe in relation to Captain Cardew than the one that Rhys occupied in her Mr Howard account. In place of the Black Exercise Book's assertion, 'I forgot about it' and the deconstruction of that assertion in the ensuing account of her dreams, the story revises that ending so that it opens out into a girl's apprehension of the strangeness and excitement of growing up. Lying alone on the flat roof in the darkness when the rest of the family have gone to see the Cardews off, Phoebe adopts a distanced view of her encounter, trying in her childish way to make sense of it by placing it in some familiar frame of reference. There is still her unquestioning acceptance of Captain Cardew's authority and judgment:

> She began to wonder how he had been so sure . . . that could only mean that he'd seen at once that she was not a good girl – who would object – but a wicked one – who would listen. He must know. He knew. It was so. (*SIOL*, p.29)

Failing to see that it was her innocence and not her sinfulness that he recognised, she proceeds to speculate from this (false) premise about what it feels like to be 'wicked': 'It was like wearing a dress that was much too big for her, a dress that swallowed her up' (*SIOL*, p.29).

It is the girl's childishness and inexperience that is plainest here as she strives to think about wickedness for women, constructing a theoretical concept based on her teaching by the nuns at the convent, where unstated connections are made between lovemaking, chastity and marriage, in opposition to which she positions herself and her feelings of 'vague irreparable loss.' Suddenly she sees herself as an outsider, separated from the familiar social scripts of feminine futures. The form Phoebe's rejection takes shows her wobbling between being 'very wise, very grown up' and very childish, as she dissociates herself from the conventional feminine hopes of marriage, trousseau lists and children's names. Phoebe says goodbye to her own favourite names, bidding them a formal farewell as she had to Captain Cardew. Instead she contemplates the difficult prospects of being different, indicating without quite realising it the subtle effect of the Captain's stories. It is indeed a 'mental seduction' as Rhys described her own experience with Mr Howard. She herself never seems to have recovered from that encounter, which was for her the ur-narrative of male–female relations, but the short story is rinsed of the pains of future knowledge by Phoebe's childish innocence:

> Now goodbye Marcus. Goodbye Rose. The prospect before her might be difficult and uncertain but it was far more exciting. (*SIOL*, p.30)

## *'The Day they Burned the Books'*

'The Day they Burned the Books', another Caribbean childhood story, also employs the narrative device of a twelve-year-old girl's limited point of view, this time to investigate two other very fraught issues for Rhys – her paranoia about women writers and the Caribbean issue of suppressed black hostility to whites. Both are encoded in the powerful image of a book-burning. Though this event is at the centre of the story, it only serves to highlight the problematic conditions of colonial discourse for colonials themselves in a hybridised culture and their ambivalent relation to inherited European traditions.

The narrative develops as the account of a friendship between the white narrator and Eddie Sawyer, the son of an Englishman and a coloured woman, and centres on the shocking event of Eddie's confrontation with his mother when she destroys his dead father's library. By its accumulation of seemingly incidental details the story presents an account of a colonial education, where cultural conditioning in the values of Englishness is always met by scepticism on the part of its white colonial inheritors and by hostility on the part of the blacks. If Eddie and the narrator scorn daffodils and strawberries and regard the real English as 'they', they are also outraged by Mrs Sawyer's outburst as she sets fire to her late husband's most cherished possessions to which her son is the inheritor: ' "My room," Eddie called it. "My books," he would say, "my books." (*TABL*, p.41)

From the *Encyclopaedia Britannica* to the poems of Milton and Byron, the list of book titles to be sold or 'burnt – yes burnt' represent those imperialist values which have oppressed Mrs Sawyer for so long. But at the moment when she seizes power, she has to face another confrontation, this time with her son, in an outburst which encodes the mutual hostility between black and white that is the tangled inheritance of this hybridised colonial culture. Eddie assumes his father's attitudes and his father's sneer as he gives his mother a violent push and snatches a book out of her hand. The encounter ends with the children each snatching a book and running outside to comfort each other under the mango tree. The confusion and pain for which they have no words is delicately imaged in the landscape itself: 'It was a red sunset that evening, a huge, sad, frightening sunset' (*TABL*, p.46).

In this story, where books are the most important objects, there are other books as well – two that survive the burning and one that does not – which are of crucial significance. The book that does not survive, although it is 'good-looking' like the ones that are to be sold rather than burnt is by a woman:

> But a book by Christina Rossetti, though also bound in leather, went into the heap that was to be burnt, and by a flicker in Mrs Sawyer's eyes I knew that worse than men who wrote books were women who wrote books – infinitely worse. Men could be mercifully shot; women must be tortured. (*TABL*, p.44)

In this striking image of an *auto da fé* is encoded a hatred of literary women that transcends the boundaries of race and gender, and for which no explanation is offered. It resonates as a peculiarly painful image of the woman writer's persecution. The books that are rescued by the children are Kipling's *Kim* and a novel by Maupassant, representing the two imperial cultures to which the children are inheritors: the Kipling is torn and the French novel looks dull. For the girl who had looked forward to her book, knowing that 'this book was the most important thing that had ever happened to me' (*TABL*, p.46) it is a terrible disappointment, and the moment of epiphany signalled by the title in the final sentence escapes her. For the adult narrator writing at a distance in time, however, the book is indeed important: it is Maupassant's *Fort Comme La Mort*, and the story testifies to its importance by being itself a revision of that novel from a colonial perspective.

The allusion to that novel allows the narrator to position herself against Mrs Sawyer, writing back to her act of violence from the authority of an inherited European literary tradition, encoding her status as a white Creole against Mrs Sawyer's black hostility. (This is a position similar to the one which Spivak comments on in Rhys's treatment of Christophine in *Wide Sargasso Sea*.[27]) The Maupassant title signals a shift of emphasis from the destruction to the survival of a literary tradition, though within the compromised circumstances of colonial inheritance. Rhys's story, like its French model, is about fetishistic objects and an *ideé fixe* which effects a transference of feeling from one person to another and which attests to the power of the past to resurrect itself in the present. Whereas Maupassant wrote about a painting and the painter's infatuation with the daughter of the subject of his picture in a story which combined love with illusion, Rhys's story is about hatred and Mrs Sawyer's desire to revenge herself on the father through the son by destroying the library which is the father's legacy. As it writes in the entanglements of the Caribbean situation, the story poses the question, what is the white Creole child heir to in the Caribbean? Is it to damaged goods and mutual hatred, and how far can this painful and complex inheritance be accommodated within the forms of European literary conventions?

## *'Temps Perdi'*

'Temps Perdi' represents Rhys's most complex questioning of her Caribbean inheritance, told in a decentred narrative which moves from the present in England at the time of World War II back to the past in Vienna immediately post World War I, and then further back to the Caribbean in a series of displaced memory fragments. The story asks what liberation from colonisation of the mind is available to a post-colonial narrator beyond the probing of received dimensions of imperial history? With its mixing of gender and international power politics, it does not offer any single answer and its doubleness is signalled in its very title, the translation of which is given at the beginning of the third section of the story:

> Temps Perdi is Creole patois and does not mean, poetically, lost or forgotten time, but, matter-of-factly, wasted time, lost labour. (*PMS*, p.81)

This title with its distinctively Caribbean inflection hovers over the loosely articulated body of multiple narrative segments, whose only connection would seem to be via the narrator's processes of memory association. There are gaps between the segments which leave room for more meanings than are ever formulated, as the present is viewed through the past in a shifting series of perspectives. The story ends when the narrator decides to write up 'Temps Perdi', the name of the ruined house in Dominica on the mirror inside the square red brick house where she is staying during the war. 'Rolvenden', the name of that English house, carries within it the idea of 'revolving' which echoes the windings of this narrative of memory. It also contains the echo of 'ending' in its threat to impose limits and silence: 'It will certainly defeat me' (*PMS*, p.73).

This is a story of colonial and female resistance to oppression which acknowledges the dialectic between oppressor and oppressed within the political realities of history. Isolated in a country house in England, the narrator harks back to Vienna in the 1920s and her experiences there with the members of the Japanese Trade Commission, remarking critically on their imperialist military ethic and their contemptuous attitude to white people and especially to women. She then turns to the history of Caribbean colonisation, focused through her more recent memory of a visit home to Dominica in the 1930s.[28] Her visit to the Carib Quarter and her encounter with the beautiful crippled Creole presents a powerful emblem of colonial submission and disablement, for the girl herself is the living embodiment of the region's forgotten history of racial and sexual oppression. Mistakenly identified as a 'Carib', she is in fact the illegitimate daughter of an unknown Frenchman and a black Martinican woman who had gone 'in service to Paris' but returned home to look after her mother. Now the girl sits mutely smiling, to be gazed at and photographed by tourists in a house in the Carib Quarter, surrounded by the trappings of European Christianity. The girl 'smiled again. And all the Virgins and saints on the walls smiled at us too' (*PMS*, p.87). She is one of the picture postcard images of Dominica in which the island's tragic history is concealed. On that varicoloured island the earth itself is a more faithful recorder than any photograph:

> Now I am home, where the earth is sometimes red and sometimes black. Round about here it is ochre – a Carib skin. In some lights like blood, in others just pretty, like a picture postcard coloured by somebody with a child's paintbox and no imagination. (*PMS*, p.88)

It is only at night after 'a good tot of rum' that the narrator can piece together the disparate elements within the Dominican historical and political situation, though the connection between them can only be focused obliquely through a half-forgotten folk song: 'the sun, the flamboyance, the girl crawling (because she could not walk) across the floor to be photographed. And the song about the white-cedar trees' (*PMS*, p.88). That song in patois ('nobody sings these old songs any more') contains within it traces of the secret female language which, the narrator notes, the nineteenth century English historian, James Froude, reported to exist among the Caribs. However, theirs is one of the lost histories of the victims of European colonisation. The song encodes that conquest too, for when the daughter asks, 'Why do the flowers last only a day?' the mother answers, 'One day and a thousand years are the same for the Bon Dieu.' (*PMS*, p.88). Really this is no answer but a statement of helpless acquiescence, where dissent is absorbed into the coloniser's patriarchal mystery of 'le Bon Dieu.'

In order to see this story as counter-discourse, it is necessary to read its statement of resistance not in its historical catalogue of events but in its structure, for the decentred narrative may be seen to be both the result of subjection to colonisation and a challenge to it. In its series of anecdotes it dismantles imperialist fictions of centrality, insisting instead on the cultural relativity of values. This story contains a multiplicity of centres, suggesting that anywhere – England, Vienna, Dominica – is marginal to somewhere else and so can be denigrated when seen through a different frame of reference. The solid English house might be only a negative when looked at through the eyes of the Creole narrator; in Vienna, European culture was held in contempt by the Japanese, German culture looked 'provincial' to the French, while the Japanese were not taken seriously by the Europeans. In the shift to the Caribbean perspective, all European conquest is seen against the backdrop of a particular colonial society with its own history of slaughter and dispossession where imperialism itself might be emblematised by the Temps Perdi Estate. 'There is no penny and no slot' here, for where is the centre when one is speaking from the Caribbean periphery with its collective memory of multiple conquests – Spanish, French, English?[29]

And what is the narrator's own position in this fabric of contradictory discourses? She aligns herself with the victims of history. Like the Caribs she is in hiding and like the Creole girl she is helpless and silenced. All she can do to register her dissent is to write up her patois message 'Temps Perdi' on the mirror in 'enemy territory' and hope that somebody might see it and be able to understand it. The very mode of resistance chosen shows a feminine preference for indeterminacy over imperial narratives of progress and mastery, in a story whose drifting meanings cannot be repressed or contained but continue to revolve after its ending.

## *'I Spy a Stranger'*

If 'Temps Perdi' is Rhys's most complex exploration of the colonial condition, then that other late wartime story, 'I Spy a Stranger,' is her sharpest critique of gender persecution as it focuses on male metanarratives of war and power and the ways in which these exclude and punish women. In both stories it is women who are the 'strangers', and when paired together they offer a wide historical perspective on the connections between patriarchal ideology, imperialism, gender conflict and colonial disablement.[30] 'I Spy a Stranger' does not have the same kind of redundancy as 'Temps Perdi' in its range of representative victims; instead it is a sharply focused investigation of the brutal mechanics of 'othering' in an English social context at a time of national crisis. It is a story of the persecution of an Englishwoman called Laura who has returned home from Europe because of the war. Instead of being granted shelter, she is suspected of being a spy, apprehended by the police for disobeying black-out regulations, and finally put away in an institution for the insane by her male persecutor, the husband of the woman who offered her lodgings in the first place.

The story makes its grim protest by a technique of double exposure as Mrs Hudson reconstructs her cousin Laura's story for her sister, Mrs Trant, interweaving into her conversation fragments from Laura's notebooks which offer the victim's perspective on events. Mrs Hudson's account is itself riddled with contradictions as she tries to justify to her sister the unjust treatment of Laura to which she has been an unwilling accomplice, at the same time as she bears witness to a process of social and marital intimidation where she too has been a victim. What emerges as the main point of the narrative is that domestic war between the sexes is as desperate and as potentially violent as the military confrontation between England and Germany.

As an outsider with a wider perspective on events in Europe than is likely to be found in the village of Malvern, Laura has set out to challenge English ideological myths about women and war at a time when such myths are being most aggressively defended. The point is made that it is her outspoken criticism of English male arrogance rather than her comments on the war itself which are regarded as most subversive. She knows that her protests are as effective as throwing herself against a brick wall, and it is plain from the conversation between Mrs Hudson and Mrs Trant that these women share that knowledge too. Mrs Hudson says, 'It's no use thinking you can ignore public opinion, because you can't' (*PMS*, p.55) and Mrs Trant comments, 'a girl ought to play safe, ought to go with the tide' (*PMS*, p.61). The only acceptable behaviour for an Englishwoman is to conform to social convention and when faced with offensive remarks about members of her own sex to 'smile and change the subject' (*PMS*, p.56). But Laura has lost her English sense of humour, and the outcome of her confrontatory tactics is predictable. Indeed, it has been predicted by Laura herself in her notebook, *No one can go against the spirit of a country with impunity*' (*PMS*, p.60). She is generally regarded as mad (although the village doctor refuses to certify her), and she is taken away to a sanatorium in the north of England, 'a large ugly house with small windows, those on the two top floors barred (*PMS*, p.66). The shadowy parallel with Thornfield Hall suggests the double fates of Laura and Antoinette. Patriarchal society has suppressed Laura as a dissident in the interests of maintaining order, and this act is rationalised as a security measure at a time of war hysteria. The whole shabby rationale is thrown into question when the story is told from the feminine point of view.

It is Laura's exercise book, confiscated and defaced by the police and left behind after her departure, that is the strongest witness to her resistance and her eventual breakdown. Though she has been silenced, her written words remain, for Mrs Hudson has kept the book despite her husband's advice to destroy it. The italicised passages from the exercise book contain Laura's most outspoken ideological critique, for she sees the social conditioning of women in England as 'propaganda' (in the same way as war propaganda) and her list of imaginary book titles is a devastating exposure of the underlying connections between sexual politics and the war mentality:

> *Woman as Obstacle to the Insect Civilization? The Standardization of Woman. The Mechanization of Woman . . . Misogyny and War. The Misery of Woman and the Evil in Men or the Great Revenge that Makes all the other Revenges Look Silly.* (*PMS*, p.60)
>
> 'Do you know,' said Mrs Hudson,' there are moments – don't laugh – when I see what she meant? All very exaggerated, of course.' (*PMS*, p.60)

The voices of female protest and feminine complicity continue in dialogue till the end, where Mrs Hudson's wish for Laura's welfare, 'Let's hope', is already undercut by the words in the exercise book, '*A forlorn hope*' (*PMS*, p.58). There is no hope for Laura, who is one of the casualties of war, a refugee from the war in Europe who is destroyed by the war between the sexes at home.[31]

In the village of Malvern, 'the gas meter's a shilling in the slot' (*PMS*, p.57), and just as Laura resisted the mechanical imposition of arbitrary classifications till her voice was suppressed, so does Rhys continue to state her resistance to the 'penny in the slot' mentality in her late short stories. Her narrators speak from Rhys's own doubly marginal position – as a white Creole woman in the Caribbean, as a colonial woman in Europe – and her narratives expose the cultural myths of two societies, a metropolitan and a colonial one, by telling the story from the perspective of those 'others' who live on the periphery of the social order. By suggesting a different representation of social and political relationships, these stories question conventional assumptions as they insist on accommodating the elements that any system excludes.

# *Conclusion*

It is really in her late stories that Rhys releases all the contradictory voices which have echoed through her fiction for over forty years, as she moves away from novel-length narratives about women cast adrift into these multivoiced fragmented discourses from the margins. These stories represent a kind of unravelling of the textures of her earlier fictions, as elements previously confined to the subtext become the substance of the main text where they are exposed as the factors through which an alienated female subjectivity is constituted. With their tendency to focus on the negative aspects of women's experience of silencing and exclusion from positions of power, such narratives are constructed out of the processes of dismantling and dissent. Yet there is a space beyond dissent, to which Rhys retreated in her old age. She refers to it as being 'like a cave at the back of your mind where you can retire and be alone and safe. The outside world is very far away. You sometimes long for a fierce dog to guard your cave'.[1] It is in the charting of that private inner territory occupied by the lone subject that Rhys makes her final contribution to a poetics of female space, and it is with two pieces spoken from those borderlines with their ghosts and shadows that I wish to end my Rhys narrative. The short story, 'I Used to Live Here Once' represents the return home to the Caribbean told through the disembodied voice of the dead,[2] and a wry late autobiographical essay, 'My Day' contains within it the briefest most frightening ghost story Rhys ever told.[3] It seems fitting to end with two images of the alienated female condition: one of a woman on the margins, and one of a woman shut in with her deepest fears.

'I Used to Live Here Once' focuses through its title on the speaking subject, but the first word of the story has shifted disconcertingly to 'she': 'She was standing by the river looking at the stepping stones and remembering each one' (*SIOL*, p.175). In this longed-for moment of return all the details of the home place are lovingly recognised by the remembering consciousness: the river, the paved road, 'the worn stone steps that led up to the house,' while the changes are registered too: 'It was strange to see a car standing in front of the house.' Yet when 'she' calls out to the children playing under the mango tree they do not answer and they do not see her. Then comes the moment of rejection and with it the moment of revelation:

> It was the boy who turned. His grey eyes looked straight into hers. His expression didn't change. He said: 'Hasn't it gone cold all of a sudden. D'you notice? Let's go in.' 'Yes let's,' said the girl.
>
> Her arms fell to her sides as she watched them running across the grass to the house. That was the first time she knew. (*SIOL*, p.176)

'She' is a ghost without knowing it.

This story figures the ultimate condition of unbelonging, for the speaking, remembering subject has no position from which her voice can be heard nor from which she can be seen. 'She' has become a woman blanked out and repositioned outside the space which was formerly her own. With its mixture of 'she' and 'I', the narrative registers a painful split between identity and subjectivity, for identity is here construed as a relational definition imposed by others, while subjectivity is an infinitely complex structure constituted of memory, desire and language which eludes any identity definition. As Rhys represents it, subjectivity might arguably survive that loss of identity which death implies, for this subject does not even 'know' that she is dead until she experiences the responses of others to her. In this strange story is coded a subtle analysis of that blankness which has always characterised Rhys's version of the feminine, where blankness is revealed to be only another face – the faceless face – of a projected identity. And again the woman's voice survives, to be heard only within the silence of textual space.

'My Day' is an old woman's account of the *faits divers* of her uneventful life, though it ends like a classic modernist short story with a moment of revelation which hollows out the spaces of that cave 'where you can retire and be alone and safe'. The narrating 'I' is alone but she is locked into a haunted house, 'alone together' with her old familiar voices in a demonic version of romantic fantasy which is pure domestic Gothic:

> When I first came here I always left my door open because I had nothing to steal and he'd always remark: 'You ought to be more careful. There're a lot of strangers about now.' Though I knew perfectly well that he and his wife call people from the next village strangers, his repeated warnings had an effect. Now I always lock up though thinking sometimes of that very frightening ghost story about the solitary woman who's just turned the key and shot the bolt for the night when she hears a voice behind her saying: 'Now we are alone together.'

# Notes

## Notes to the Introduction

1. I am grateful for the resources of the Jean Rhys Collection in the Department of Special Collections, McFarlin Library, University of Tulsa, Oklahoma, and the Manuscripts Department of the British Library, whose collections of unpublished Rhys material have been crucially important in the construction of this narrative.
2. As I am concerned primarily with Rhys's fiction, the following review of criticism does not include biographical studies by David Plante, *Difficult Women: A Memoir of Three* (London: Gollancz, 1983) and Carole Angier, *Jean Rhys* (Harmondsworth: Penguin, 1985). Angier's full biography *Jean Rhys* (London: Deutsch, 1990) appeared after my typescript was completed.
3. Louis James, *Jean Rhys* (London: Longman, 1978).
4. Wally Look Lai, 'The Road to Thornfield Hall,' *New Beacon Reviews* 1968, pp.38–52; V. S. Naipaul, 'Without a Dog's Chance,' *New York Review of Books*, 18 May 1972, p.28; John Hearne, 'The *Wide Sargasso Sea*: A West Indian Reflection,' *Cornhill Magazine*, 180 (Summer 1974), pp.323–33.
5. Thomas F. Staley, *Jean Rhys: A Critical Study* (London: Macmillan, 1970).
6. *ibid*, pp.52–3.
7. Helen Nebeker, *Jean Rhys, Woman in Passage: A Critical Study* (Montreal: Eden Press, 1981).
8. *ibid*, p.199.
9. Gayatri Spivak, 'Three Women's Texts and a Critique of Imperialism,' *Critical Inquiry*, 12, Autumn 1985, pp.243–61; Helen Tiffin, 'Post-Colonial Literatures and Counter-Discourses,' *Kunapipi*, 9, 3, 1987, pp.17–34.

10. Teresa F. O'Connor, *Jean Rhys's West Indian Novels* (New York and London: New York University Press, 1986).
11. *ibid*, p.10.
12. Nancy R. Harrison, *Jean Rhys and the Novel as Women's Text* (Chapel Hill and London: University of North Carolina Press, 1988); Deborah Kelly Kloepfer, *The Unspeakable Mother: Forbidden Discourse in Jean Rhys and H.D.* (Ithaca and London: Cornell University Press, 1989).
13. Nancy R. Harrison, *op. cit.*, p.63.
14. Shari Benstock, *Women of the Left bank: Paris 1900–1940* (Austin: University of Texas Press, 1986).
15. Sandra Gilbert and Susan Gubar, *No Man's Land: The Place of the Woman Writer in the Twentieth Century*, vol. 2 (New Haven: Yale University Press, 1989).
16. Bonnie Kime Scott (ed.) *The Gender of Modernism: A Critical Anthology* (Bloomington and Indianapolis: Indiana University Press, 1990).

## *Notes to Chapter One*

1. *Jean Rhys: Letters, 1931–1966*, edited by Francis Wyndham and Diana Melly (London: Andre Deutsch, 1984), p.65, 6 December 1949, to Peggy Kirkaldy.
2. Jean Rhys, *Smile Please* (London: Deutsch, 1979), p.163.
3. David Plante, 'Jean Rhys: A Remembrance,' *Paris Review* 76 (1979), pp.238–58; and *JRL*, p.103.
4. Elizabeth Vreeland, 'Jean Rhys: The Art of Fiction' *Paris Review* 76 (1979), pp.219–37.
5. 'I Spy a Stranger' (1966), repr. in *Penguin Modern Stories* (Harmondsworth: Penguin, 1969).
6. *JRL*, p.261. A poem 'Obeah Night' is attached to this letter, and seven poems by Rhys are in the Jean Rhys Collection 1:13, University of Tulsa.
7. Rosalind Coward, 'Are Women's Novels Feminist Novels?' in *The New Feminist Criticism*, edited by Elaine Showalter (London: Virago, 1986), pp.225–39.
8. Luce Irigaray, *Speculum de l'autre femme* (Paris: Minuit, 1974). Irigaray's arguments about women's relation to sexuality and desire are astutely analysed by Jane Gallop, *The Daughter's Seduction: Feminism and Psychoanalysis* (Ithaca: Cornell, 1982), and I am much indebted to Chapter 5 'The Father's Seduction' in my construction of parallels between the critiques of Freud offered by Irigaray and Rhys.
9. Rachel Blau Du Plessis, *Writing Beyond the Ending: Narrative Strategies of Twentieth-Century Women Writers* (Bloomington: Indiana University Press, 1985).
10. Rosalind Coward, *Female Desire* (London: Paladin, 1984); and Nancy

K.Miller, 'Emphasis Added: Plots and Plausibilities in Women's Fiction,' (1981), repr, in *The New Feminist Criticism op. cit.*, pp.339–60.
11. Alice Munro, 'Bardon Bus,' *The Moons of Jupiter* (Toronto: Macmillan, 1982).
12. The Mr Howard material comes from the Black Exercise Book held in the Jean Rhys Collection 1:1, University of Tulsa. Written by Rhys in the late 1930s, it has no pagination, and my transcription leaves Rhys's unpunctuated drafts intact. O'Connor refers to the Mr Howard story, but she does not accord it the central importance in Rhys's personal mythology that I wish to do.
13. Rhys's account accurately paraphrases, with one important variant, Freud's remarks on female hysterics' fantasies of seduction by the father in 'Femininity' (1933), *Complete Psychological Works of Sigmund Freud*, vol. 22 (London: Hogarth Standard Edition, 1964), p.120.
14. Jane Gallop, *The Daughter's Seduction: Feminism and Psychoanalysis* (Ithaca: Cornell, 1982), pp. 56–79.
15. Jane Gallop, *op. cit.*, p.16.
16. Luce Irigaray, *Speculum de l'autre femme*, p.61, quoted in J. Gallop. *op cit.*, p.70.
17. Jane Gallop, *op. cit.*, p.71.
18. *ibid*, p.78.
19. *ibid*, p.79.
20. Judith Kegan Gardiner, 'On Female Identity and Writing by Women,' in ed., E. Abel, *Writing and Sexual Difference* (Brighton: Harvester, 1982), pp.177–92.
21. Jean Rhys, 'Leaving School: How I Became a Novelist,' undated ms. draft c.1974, Jean Rhys Collection 1:28, University of Tulsa.
22. B. Ashcroft, G. Griffiths, H. Tiffin, *The Empire Writes Back: Theory and Practice in Post-Colonial Literatures* (London: Routledge, New Accents, 1989), p.9.
23. Alec Waugh, *The Sugar Islands* (London: Cassell, 1958), p.309.
24. Elaine Campbell, 'An Expatriate at Home: Dominica's Elma Napier,' *Kunapipi*, 4, 1 (1982), pp.82–93.
25. Wally Look Lai, *op. cit.*, 'The Road to Thornfield Hall,' pp.38–52.
26. Edward Brathwaite, *Contradictory Omens* (Mona, Jamaica: Savacou Publications, 1974). I am grateful to John Thieme for this reference.
27. Jean Rhys, *Wide Sargasso Sea* (London: Andre Deutsch,1966), p.102.
28. Black Exercise Book, Jean Rhys Collection 1:1, University of Tulsa.
29. For detailed historical accounts of the plantation system, see Eric Williams, *From Columbus to Castro: The History of the Caribbean, 1492–1969* (London: Andre Deutsch, 1970); F. W. Knight, *The Caribbean: The Genesis of a Fragmented Nationalism* (New York: OUP, 1978); and Philip D. Curtin, *The Rise and Fall of the Plantation Complex: Essays in Atlantic History* (Cambridge: Cambridge University Press, 1990).

30. Alec Waugh, *op. cit.*, p.282; Rhys, 'The Imperial Road,' Jean Rhys Collection, 1:24., University of Tulsa.
31. S. Slemon, 'Monuments of Empire: Allegory, Counter-Discourse, Post-Colonial Writing, '*Kunapipi*, 9, 3 (1987), pp.1–16.
32. Gayatri Spivak, *op. cit.*, p.249.
33. See Andreas Huyssen, *After the Great Divide: Modernism, Mass Culture, Postmodernism* (Bloomington: Indiana UP, 1986); Steven Connor, *Postmodernist Culture: An Introduction to Theories of the Contemporary* (Oxford: Blackwell, 1989); Shari Benstock, *Women of the Left Bank: Paris 1900–1940* (Austin: University of Texas Press, 1986); and Bonnie Kime Scott (ed.), *The Gender of Modernism: A Critical Anthology* (Bloomington: Indiana University Press, 1990).
34. Standard masculine critical studies of modernism include B. Bergonzi, *The Myth of Modernism and Twentieth Century Literature* (Brighton: Harvester, 1986); M. Bradbury and J. MacFarlane (eds.), *Modernism 1880–1930* (London: Penguin, 1976); C. K. Stead, *Pound, Yeats, Eliot and the Modernist Movement* (London: Macmillan, 1985); and J. Symons, *Makers of the New: The Revolution in Literature, 1912–1939* (London: Andre Deutsch, 1987).
35. This phrase appears in the unpublished letter, Jean Rhys Collection 3:13, University of Tulsa, though not in the published version.
36. Among numerous revisionist studies of female urban modernism, see Susan M. Squier, *Virginia Woolf and London: Sexual Politics of the City* (Chapel Hill and London: University of N. Carolina Press, 1985); and S. Benstock, *op. cit.*, pp.433–50.
37. 'After Leaving School: How I Became a Novelist,' Jean Rhys Collection 1:28, University of Tulsa.

## *Notes to Chapter Two*

1. Jean Rhys Collection 1:28, University of Tulsa. Having compared the original handwritten version with Mary Lou Emery's typed transcript annotated by Rhys, I quote from the typed version which, unlike the original, is punctuated.
2. Letter to Isabel Paterson, 5 March 1928, *Letters of Ford Madox Ford*, ed. R. M. Ludwig (Princeton: Princeton UP, 1965).
3. Judith Kegan Gardiner, 'Rhys Recalling Ford: *Quartet* and *The Good Soldier*', *Tulsa Studies in Women's Literature*, 1, 1, (1982), pp.67–81.
4. *The Left Bank and Other Stories* (1927). Page references are to the Books for Libraries Press Reprint, 1970. This volume was never republished, though a selection of the stories appeared in *Tigers Are Better-Looking*.
5. Michel Foucault, 'The Order of Discourse,' (1972), repr. in *Untying the Text*, edited by R. Young (London: Routledge & Kegan Paul, 1981), pp.48–78.

6. *Times Literary Supplement*, 5 May 1927, p.320. This was the same issue in which *To the Lighthouse* was reviewed.
7. P. Hochstadt, 'From Vulnerability to Selfhood: the pain-filled affirmations of Jean Rhys', *Jean Rhys Review*, 2, 1,(1987), pp.2–6.
8. A. Borinsky, 'Jean Rhys: Poses of a Woman as Guest,' in *The Female Body in Western Culture*, edited by Susan Sulieman (Mass: Harvard UP, 1986), pp.288–302.
9. Veronica Gregg, 'Jean Rhys and Modernism: A Different Voice', *Jean Rhys Review*, 1, 2, (1987), pp.30–46.
10. H. Tiffin, 'Post-Colonial Literature and Counter-Discourse', *op. cit.*, p.19.
11. The significance of the name Roseau, capital of Dominica, is disguised here where the protagonist explains her name as meaning 'a reed', situating it in relation to La Fontaine's fable, 'Le Chêne et le Roseau'.
12. I am indebted to Professor Annie Escuret of Université Paul Valery, Montpellier, for pointing out the parallels between the Rhys and the Maupassant stories.
13. Likewise, I am indebted for this identification to Professor Annie Escuret and to Professor Paule Plouvier. *Le Livre pour toi* appeared in its 42nd edition, with a Preface by Henri Bataille (Paris: A. Michel) in 1926; this is likely to be the edition that Rhys used.
14. 'Vienne' is the only story to be modified in those reprinted from *The Left Bank* in *Tigers Are Better-Looking*.
15. Toril Moi, *Sexual/Textual Politics* (London: Methuen, 1985), p.150.
16. Green Exercise Book, Jean Rhys Collection 1:2, University of Tulsa.
17. Martien Kappers-den Hollander, 'A Gloomy Child and Its Devoted Godmother: *Barred, Sous les Verrous* and *In de Strik*', in *Autobiographical and Biographical Writing in the Commonwealth*, edited by D. MacDermott (Barcelona, Editorial AUSA 1984), pp.123–30.
18. Martien Kappers-den Hollander, 'Measure for Measure: *Quartet* and *When the Wicked Man*,' *Jean Rhys Review*, 2, 2 (Spring 1988), pp.2–17.
19. *ibid*, p.6
20. *ibid*, p.5
21. *ibid*, p.5
22. Discussed by M. K. Hollander, 'A Gloomy Child,' *op.cit.* p.124.
23. Letter to Oliver Stoner, 24 April 1968, Jean Rhys Collection 3:14, University of Tulsa. This dating would seriously challenge Gardiner's hypothesis that *Quartet* was writing back to *The Good Soldier*.
24. Diana Athill's Foreword to *Smile Please*, *op. cit.*, pp.9–10.
25. The names of the main characters suggest a version of the *roman à clef* combined with a morality play. 'Heidler' a German name (associated with 'heiler': healer and 'Heiland': Saviour) recalls that Ford's real name was 'Hueffer'; Lois (associated with 'Lux': light) links with 'Stella' Bowen; Marya, nicknamed 'Mado' recalls the Rhys figure's ambiguous status between the Virgin Mary and

Madeleine the fallen woman; Stephan Zelli (the Lenglet figure) is a doublefaced name, associated with martyrdom but also with espionage: 'Zelle' was the surname of the Mata Hari, the Dutch-born dancer and courtesan who was shot as a German spy in 1917.

26. *New York Herald Tribune*, 10 February 1929, p.8.
27. Jean Rhys, *Quartet* (London: Deutsch, 1969), p.14.
28. Judith Kegan Gardiner, 'On Female Identity and Writing by Women,' *op. cit.*, p.180.
29. For a fascinating exploration of this territory of finding definition as the 'other' and moving through different forms of victimisation, see Sue Roe, 'The Shadow of Light: The Symbolic Underworld of Jean Rhys', in ed., Sue Roe, *Women Reading Women's Writing*, (Brighton: Harvester, 1987), pp.229–64.
30. Ann Snitow, 'Mass Market Romance: Pornography for women is different', in ed., A. Snitow *et al'*, *Desire: the Politics of Sexuality*, (London: Virago, 1984), pp. 258–75.
31. Rhys uses the Rasputin image again in a letter to Selma Vaz Dias, 27 October 1956, *JRL*, p.136.

## Notes to Chapter Three

1. Deborah Kelly Kloepfer, *The Unspeakable Mother: Forbidden Discourse in Jean Rhys and H.D.* (Ithaca & London: Cornell University Press,1989), p.59.
2. *Times Literary Supplement*, 5 March 1931, p.180.
3. Jean Rhys, *After Leaving Mr Mackenzie* (London: Deutsch, 1969), p.10.
4. Virginia Woolf, *To the Lighthouse* (Harmondsworth: Penguin, 1964), p.165.
5. David Lodge, *The Modes of Modern Writing* (London: Arnold, 1977), p.179.
6. British Library, ADD MS 57856, p.5.
7. Rachel Bowlby, *Virginia Woolf: Feminist Destinations* (Oxford: Blackwell, 1988), p.62–79; and Pierre Bourdieu, 'He whose word is law,' *Liber*, 1, 1 (1989), pp.12–13, in the *Times Literary Supplement*, October 1989.
8. I disagree with Nancy Hemond Brown, 'On Becoming a Butterfly: Issues of Identity in *After Leaving Mr Mackenzie*,' *Jean Rhys Review*, 2, 1 (1987), pp.6–15, where she argues that this novel is a quest for identity. However, it seems that telling her life story is for Julia more a deconstructive than a constructive exercise.
9. D. K. Kloepfer, *op. cit.* argues persuasively for the crucial importance of absent mothers in Rhys's fiction, and I refer here to her discussion of this novel in chap. 3, pp.46–62.
10. British Library, ADD MS 57856, p.5.
11. D. K. Kloepfer, *op. cit.*, p.61.

12. This unconventional aspect is noted by at least one contemporary reviewer. Margaret Cheyney Dawson in *New York Herald Tribune Books* (28 June 1931), p.7, says, 'This is the only novel on this subject that does not drag death in by the tail to supply a strong climax'.
13. Rachel Blau Du Plessis, *Writing Beyond the Ending: Narrative Strategies in Twentieth Century Women Writers* (Bloomington: Indiana U. Press, 1985).
14. Quoted from Helen Nebeker, *Jean Rhys: Woman in Passage*, by Nancy Hemond Brown, *op. cit.*, p.14, n.5.

## *Notes to Chapter Four*

1. Jean Rhys, *Voyage in the Dark* (1934) (London: Deutsch, 1967), pp.187–8. I quote from the published ending where Anna survives her abortion; in the original unpublished ending she dies. In either case she is effectively silenced; whether temporarily or permanently depends on which ending one is referring to.
2. Michael Dash, 'In Search of the Lost Body: Redefining the subject in Caribbean Literature,' *Kunapipi*, 11, 1 (1989), pp.17–26.
3. (eds.) K. Holst Petersen & A. Rutherford, *A Double Colonisation: Colonial and Post-Colonial Women's Writing*, (Aarhus: Dangaroo Press, 1986).
4. *JRL*, pp.277–8, 14 May 1964, to Francis Wyndham.
5. Carole Angier, *Jean Rhys*, (Harmondsworth: Penguin, 1985), pp.33–40.
6. Jean Rhys, *Smile Please*, (London: Deutsch, 1979) p.129.
7. 'Leaving School: How I Became a Novelist,' Jean Rhys Collection 1:28, University of Tulsa.
8. *ibid.*
9. There has been much discussion among feminist critics over which ending is to be preferred, the published version or the original version now in the Jean Rhys Collection, University of Tulsa, which has been published with prefatory comments by Nancy Hemond Brown in the *London Magazine*, New Series, 25, 1 & 2 (April/May 1985), pp.40–59. See also Teresa F. O'Connor, *op. cit.*, pp.130–31; Nancy R. Harrison, *op. cit.*, pp.105–6; Deborah Kelly Kloepfer, *op. cit.*, pp.75–8. I shall discuss the two endings in the final section of this chapter.
10. Jean Rhys Collection, 1:28, University of Tulsa.
11. *JRL*, p.25, 10 June 1934, to Evelyn Scott.
12. *Saturday Review of Books*, 16 March, 1935, p.556. This review appeared after American publication in Spring 1935.
13. Letter to Oliver Stoner, 15 December, 1969, Jean Rhys Collection 3:17, University of Tulsa.
14. *JRL*, p.236, 30 August 1963, to Selma Vaz Dias.

15. Foreword to *Smile Please, op. cit.*, p.10.
16. 'How I Became a Novelist,' Jean Rhys Collection 1:28, University of Tulsa.
17. *JRL*, p.24, 10 June 1934, to Evelyn Scott.
18. This scrambling of voices from the present and the past is developed with wider resonances in the longer unpublished version of the ending.
19. *JRL*, p.24.
20. D. K. Kloepfer, *op. cit.*, pp. 63–78, discusses *Voyage in the Dark* as Rhys's most sustained exploration of the absent mother and mother surrogates.
21. Peter Brooks, *Reading for the Plot: Design and Intention in Narrative.* (Oxford: Clarendon, 1984), p.145.
22. Nancy K. Miller,' Emphasis Added: Plots and Plausibilities in Women's Fiction', in (ed.) E. Showalter *The New Feminist Criticism*, (London: Virago, 1986), pp.339–60.
23. Nancy R. Harrison, *op. cit.*, p.71–84 comments on Rhys's use of italics here to indicate a subtext within a subtext, suggesting multiple layerings of consciousness.
24. Black Exercise Book, Jean Rhys Collection 1:1, University of Tulsa.
25. Juliet Mitchell, 'Femininity, Narrative and Psychoanalysis', repr., in *Modern Criticism and Theory: A Reader*, edited by David Lodge (London & New York: Longman, 1988), pp.426–30.
26. S.Gubar, 'The Blank Page and Issues of Female Creativity', in ed., E. Abel, *Writing and Sexual Difference* (Brighton: Harvester, 1987) pp.73–94.
27. Quoted from the *London Magazine* as in n.9, above, p.56.
28. *ibid*, p.49.

## Notes to Chapter Five

1. Jean Rhys, *Good Morning, Midnight* (1939) (London: Deutsch, 1967), p.44.
2. The positioning of woman as Other is discussed in Luce Irigaray's 'This Sex Which Is Not One' and Julia Kristeva's 'Oscillation between Power and Denial', in eds., Elaine Marks & Isabelle de Courtivron, *New French Feminisms: An Anthology*, (Brighton: Harvester, 1980), pp.99–106 and pp.165–7. See also Alice Jardine, *Gynesis: Configurations of Women and Modernity* (Ithaca and London: Cornell University Press, 1985) and ed., Barbara Godard, *Gynocritics/La Gynocritique* (Toronto: ECW, 1987).
3. L. Hutcheon, *The Canadian Postmodern: A Study of Contemporary English Canadian Fiction* (Oxford: OUP, 1988), p.110.
4. Wendy Barker, *Lunacy of Light: Emily Dickinson and the Experience of Metaphor* (Carbondale: Southern Illinois University Press, 1987); and K. Keller, 'Sleeping with Emily Dickinson,' in ed., Suzanne

Juhasz *Feminist Critics Read Emily Dickinson* (Bloomington: Indiana University Press, 1983).

5. Wendy Barker, *op. cit.*, p.75.
6. Black Exercise Book, Jean Rhys Collection 1:1, University of Tulsa. This entry is written on six pages reversed at the end of the notebook, which contain fragments of *Good Morning, Midnight* drafts.
7. *New English Weekly* April 1939, and Julian Jebb's review of the reissue of the novel, *Financial Times*, 1967.
8. L. Hutcheon, *A Poetics of Postmodernism: History, Theory, Fiction* (New York & London: Routledge, 1988).
9. For different approaches to reading a character like Sasha's, see Elizabeth Abel, 'Women and Schizophrenia: The Fiction of Jean Rhys, '*Contemporary Fiction*, 20 (1979), pp.155–77; and Eve Kosofsky Sedgwick, *The Coherence of Gothic Conventions* (New York and London: Methuen, 1980), pp.97–139.
10. E. Abel, *op. cit.*, p.166.
11. The moment of male–female contact in darkness is replayed differently in *GMM* from Julia's disastrous experience with Mr Horsfield in *ALMM* giving Sasha her one moment when the past is restored to her completely.
12. Sasha displays many of the symptoms of schizophrenia documented by Abel, *op. cit.*, though I find Abel's Laingian binary model rather outdated.
13. For a feminist reading of Molly Bloom, see Suzette A. Henke, *James Joyce and the Politics of Desire*, (New York & London: Routledge, 1990), p.127.
14. See L. Hutcheon, *The Canadian Postmodern*, (Oxford: OUP, 1988) pp.107–37.
15. 'The Waste Land', *Selected Poems: T. S. Eliot* (London: Faber, 1954). Passages quoted are from 'The Fire Sermon', p.60.
16. Susan M. Squier, 'Virginia Woolf's London and the Feminist Revision of Modernism,' in (ed.) Mary Anne Caws, *City, Text, Thought*, (Gordon & Breach, 1990). I quote from the typescript.
17. Shari Benstock, *Women of the Left Bank: Paris 1900–1940* (Austin: University of Texas Press, 1986), pp.437–41. Benstock's comparison suggests another interesting dimension to Rhys's modernism in her use of expressionist techniques. For a discussion of expressionist aesthetics, see Sherrill Grace, *Regression and Apocalypse: Studies in North American Expressionism* (Toronto, Buffalo, New York: University of Toronto Press, 1989).
18. I have written more fully about this episode in my Introduction to the Jean Rhys section in ed., Bonnie Kime Scott *The Gender of Modernism* (Bloomington and Indianapolis: Indiana University Press, 1990).
19. Letter to Evelyn Scott, 18 February 1934. *JRL*, p.24.
20. Sue Roe in 'The Shadow of Light: The Symbolic Underworld of Jean Rhys', *Women Reading Women's Writing* (Brighton: Harvester,

1987), pp.250–1 offers as different interpretation of this scene, reading it as Caribbean fantasy where Sasha's persona is that of a black woman. The two interpretations suggest the degree to which elements of Rhys's repressed narratives are interwoven in her fictional constructs.

21. Black Exercise Book, Jean Rhys Collection 1:1, University of Tulsa.

# Notes to Chapter Six

1. *JRL*, p.262, 14 April 1964, to Francis Wyndham.
2. After her rediscovery by Francis Wyndham in 1957 and with his encouragement, Rhys published several short stories in the *London Magazine* in the early 1960s.
3. Wally Look Lai, 'The Road to Thornfield Hall,' *New Beacon Reviews* 1968, pp.38–52; Helen Tiffin, 'Post-colonial Literatures and Counter-Discourse,' *Kunapipi*, 9, 3, 1987, pp.17–34; Gayatri Spivak, 'Three Women's Texts and a Critique of Imperialism,' *Critical Inquiry*, 12, Autumn 1985, pp.243–61.
4. In a letter to me (9 May 1989) Carole Angier mentions this information as given to her by Leslie Tilden Smith's daughter, Mrs Phyllis Smyser, whom she had interviewed several times before her death.
5. I am indebted to John Thieme for this piece of evidence, which may well have been crucial in the genesis of *Wide Sargasso Sea*. In addition, there are two essays by Elaine Campbell which throw some light on the relationship between the novels: 'A Report from Dominica, B.W.I.,' *World Literature Written in English*, 17, 1 April 1978, pp.305–16; and her Introduction to the Virago reprint of *The Orchid House* (London, 1982).
6. Jean Rhys, 'About Work', Unpublished letter to Selma Vaz Dias, 5 October 1957, Jean Rhys Collection, 2:6, University of Tulsa.
7. G. Spivak, *op. cit.*, p.244.
8. Unpub. letter to Peggy Kirkaldy, 30 July 1957. Jean Rhys Collection, University of Tulsa, New Deutsch Files 1989; not yet catalogued. The original letter is in the possession of the Jean Rhys Estate.
9. Jean Rhys, *Wide Sargasso Sea* (London: Andre Deutsch, 1966). p.172. All references are to this edition.
10. G. Spivak, *op. cit.*, p.243.
11. G. Spivak, *op. cit.*, p.253.
12. See E. Williams, *From Columbus to Castro*, (London: Andre Deutsch, 1970) chap.17 'The Abolition of the Caribbean Slave System'; F. W. Knight, *The Caribbean* (New York: OUP, 1978) chap. 6 'Disintegration and Reconstruction 1793–1886'; and P. D. Curtin, *The Rise and Fall of the Plantation Complex*, (Cambridge: CUP, 1990) chap.13 'Readjustments in the Nineteenth Century'.

13. Mr Mason's 'new colonialism' is signalled in his plans (*WSS*, p.35) to import contract labourers from India and the East Indies to replace former slave labour. As Curtin comments, 'Between 1845 and 1914 India supplied nearly 450,000 contract workers for the British West Indies' (P. D. Curtin, *op. cit.*, p.177).
14. Teresa F. O'Connor, *Jean Rhys's West Indian Novels* (New York: New York University Press, 1986) p.184, notes the correspondence between Antoinette's second dream and the dream in the Black Exercise Book. However, it is not a verbatim account as O'Connor suggests for there are omissions and constructs in the novel version which do not feature in the original.
15. F. Jameson, 'Magical Narratives: Romance as Genre,' *New Literary History*, 7, 1, 1975, pp.135–59.
16. Elaine Campbell, 'Reflections on Obeah in Jean Rhys's Fiction,' *Kunapipi*, 4, 2 1982, pp.42–50.
17. F. Jameson, *op. cit.*, p. 146.
18. J. Thieme, 'Apparitions of Disaster: Brontëan Parallels in *Wide Sargasso Sea* and *Guerillas*,' *Journal of Commonwealth Literature*, 14, 1, 1979, pp.116–132, focuses on Antoinette's tragic predicament which is also historically a West Indian one. His essay extends the views of Louis James, Wally Look Lai and John Hearne.
19. It is to be noted that Christophine is not Jamaican; she comes from Martinique, one of the French Caribbean islands which was briefly (1794–1814) under British control. There was great fear of French influenced slave revolts in British-held Jamaica, and there may well be a political dimension to the police surveillance over her. For a history of slave unrest in the French Caribbean, see P. D. Curtin, *op. cit.*, Chap.11.
20. Luce Irigaray, *This Sex Which Is Not One*; quoted by Mary Russo in 'Female Grotesques: Carnival and Theory' in *Feminist Studies/Critical Studies* edited by Teresa de Laurentis (Bloomington: Indiana University Press, 1986), p.223.
21. W. B. Yeats, 'In Memory of Eva Gore-Booth and Con Markiewicz,' *Collected Poems* (London: Macmillan, 1967), p.264.
22. Charlotte Brontë, *Jane Eyre* (Harmondsworth: Penguin Classics, 1986), p.239–40.

## *Notes to Chapter Seven*

1. *JRL*, pp.238–9.
2. Jean Rhys, *Tigers are Better-Looking* (London: Andre Deutsch, 1968) and *Sleep It Off Lady* (London: Andre Deutsch, 1976).
3. Letter to Olwen Hughes, 28 June 1976, Jean Rhys Collection 3:6, University of Tulsa.
4. Letter to Oliver Stoner, 14 June 1975, Jean Rhys Collection 3:23, University of Tulsa.

5. For fascinating discussions of the genesis of two other stories, see C. Angier, 'Week-End in Gloucestershire: Jean Rhys and "Till September, Petronella",' the *London Magazine,* New Series, 27, 3 June 1987, pp.30–46, and Delphine Chartier, 'Jean Rhys : L'Auto-censure créatrice: Analyse des versions successives de la nouvelle "Rapunzel, Rapunzel",' *Jean Rhys Review,* 1, 1 1986, pp.15–29.
6. For dates of individual publication of Rhys's stories, see the excellent chronological list in Elgin W. Mellown, *Jean Rhys: A Descriptive and Annotated Bibliography of Works and Criticism* (New York and London: Garland, 1984).
7. First published in the *London Magazine,* New Series, 2, 1, February 1962, Repr. in *TABL.*
8. Rhys spent five days in Holloway Prison in 1949, after being found guilty of assault for slapping the face of the man upstairs at her lodgings in Kent. See *JRL,* p.57.
9. First published in the *London Magazine,* New Series, 2, 2, October 1962. Repr. in *TABL.*
10. First published in *Art and Literature,* 9, Summer 1966. Repr. in *TABL.*
11. First Published in the *New Yorker,* 52, 30 August 1976. Repr. in *SIOL.*
12. First published in the *London Magazine,* New Series, 7, July 1960. Repr. in *TABL.*
13. First published in *Art and Literature.* 12, Spring 1967. Repr. in *Penguin Modern Stories* (London: Penguin, 1969).
14. First published in *Art and Literature,* 8, Spring 1966. Repr. in *Penguin Modern Stories* (London: Penguin, 1969).
15. *SIOL,* p.155.
16. Unpublished letter dated 1949. Jean Rhys Collection, New Deutsch Files, University of Tulsa; uncatalogued. The original is in the possession of the Jean Rhys Estate.
17. One of the few essays to focus on Rhys's positive social criticism is Lucy Wilson, 'Women Must Have Spunks: Jean Rhys's Black Outcasts', *Modern Fiction Studies,* 32, 3, Autumn 1986, pp.439–48.
18. Diana Athill's description in unpublished letter to Rhys, 21 March 1967. Jean Rhys Collection, New Deutsch Files; University of Tulsa; uncatalogued.
19. The music was not always bad: George Melly tells the anecdote that during the last years of her life Rhys regularly attended his Christmas seasons at Ronnie Scott's club and even gave him some lyrics to set to music. One of them 'Life With You' is the title track on the 'Feetwarmers' latest album. (*St Pancras Chronicle,* 15 February, 1990).
20. In my thinking about carnivalesque discourse, I am indebted to R. J. Howells, *Carnival to Classicism: The Comic Novels of Charles Sorel* (Paris, Seattle, Tubingen: Biblio 17, 1989).
21. Unpublished letter, Jean Rhys Collection 3:1, C, University of Tulsa: Phyllis Smith (Mrs. R. E.) Smyser Correspondence.

22. *JRL*, p.39, October 1945, to Peggy Kirkaldy.
23. See Sherrill Grace, *Regression and Apocalypse: Studies in North American Expressionism* (Toronto and New York: University of Toronto Press, 1989) for detailed discussion of the techniques of Expressionist art.
24. Nancy Hemond Brown, 'A Comparison of Jean Rhys's "The Sound of the River" with Ernest Hemingway's "Hills Like White Elephants" ', *Jean Rhys Review*, 1, 1, 1986, pp.2–12, points to typographic signals which suggest Rhys's impressionistic register of time and the surfacing of subconscious fear in this story.
25. Charlotte Brontë, *Jane Eyre*, (Harmondsworth: Penguin Classics, 1986), p.296.
26. Jean Rhys Collection 1:16, University of Tulsa, contains four versions written between 1974 and 1976, the main changes being a shift from first to third person narrative, title change and expanded ending.
27. Spivak, *op. cit.*, p.253.
28. Rhys returned once to Dominica in 1936, when she and Leslie Tilden Smith visited the Carib reserve at Salybia.
29. See H. Hoetink, 'Race and Colour in the Caribbean', in *Caribbean Contours*, edited by S. W. Minsk and S. Price (Baltimore: Johns Hopkins, 1985), pp.55–84, for a description of the islands' multilayered racial archaeology.
30. See Nancy Casey Fulton, 'The Liberated Woman in Jean Rhys's Late Short Fiction', *Revista Americana Review*, 4, Summer 1974, pp.264–72, who sees these stories as Rhys's reappraisal of former subservient 'feminine' positions. However, this essay neglects the important element of colonial resistance.
31. In writing this section I am indebted to some of the essays in *Arms and the Woman: War, Gender and Literary Representation*, edited by H. M. Cooper, A. A. Munich and S. M. Squier (Chapel Hill and London: University of North Carolina Press,1989).

## Notes to Conclusion

1. 'Close Season for the Old?'. One of three stories in *My Day: Three Pieces by Jean Rhys*. (Vermont: Stinehour Press, 1975). I quote, with grateful acknowledgement, from the galley proofs, Jean Rhys Collection, 1:30, University of Tulsa.
2. Last story in *Sleep It Off Lady*, not published previously.
3. First published in *Vogue* 165, February 1975, and repr. as first essay in *My Day*. I quote from the corrected typescript submitted by Rhys to *Vogue*, 24 January, 1974, Jean Rhys Collection 1:22, University of Tulsa.

# *Bibliography*

## *Primary*

With four exceptions*, all references to Jean Rhys's published works in the text are to the Andre Deutsch editions of the 1960s and 70s:

*Quartet* (London: Chatto & Windus, 1928; Reissued London: Andre Deutsch, 1969).

*After Leaving Mr Mackenzie* (London: Jonathan Cape, 1930; Reissued London: Andre Deutsch, 1969).

*Voyage in the Dark* (London: Constable, 1934; Reissued London: Andre Deutsch, 1967).

*Good Morning, Midnight* (London: Constable, 1939; Reissued London: Andre Deutsch, 1967).

*Wide Sargasso Sea* (London: Andre Deutsch, 1966).

*Tigers are Better-Looking* (London: Andre Deutsch, 1968).

*Sleep It Off Lady* (London: Andre Deutsch, 1976).

*Smile Please* (London: Andre Deutsch, 1979).

*Jean Rhys: Letters,1931–1966*, edited by Francis Wyndham and Diana Melly (London: Andre Deutsch, 1984).

* *The Left Bank and Other Stories* (London: Jonathan Cape, 1927) is available in Short Story Index Reprint Series, Books for Libraries Press (New York: Arno, 1970); 'I Spy a Stranger' and 'Temps Perdi' in *Penguin Modern Stories*, (London: Penguin, 1969); and 'My Day' in *My Day: Three Pieces by Jean Rhys*. (Vermont: Stinehour Press, 1975): I have quoted from the galley proofs in the Jean Rhys Special Collection, McFarlin Library, University of Tulsa.

# Secondary

Abel, Elizabeth (ed.), *Writing and Sexual Difference* (Brighton: Harvester, 1982).

Abel, Elizabeth, 'Women and Schizophrenia: The Fiction of Jean Rhys', *Contemporary Literature*, 20, 1979, pp.155–77.

Angier, Carole, *Jean Rhys* (Harmondsworth: Penguin, 1985).

Angier, Carole, *Jean Rhys* (London: Deutsch, 1990).

Angier, Carole, 'Week-End in Gloucestershire: Jean Rhys and "Till September Petronella" ', *London Magazine*, 27,3, June 1987, pp.30–46.

Ashcroft, Bill, G.Griffiths, and H.Tiffin, *The Empire Writes Back: Theory and Practice in Post-Colonial Literatures* (London: Routledge, 1989).

Barker, Wendy, *Lunacy of Light: Emily Dickinson and the Experience of Metaphor* (Carbondale and Illinois: Southern Illinois University Press, 1987).

Benstock, Shari, *Women of the Left Bank: Paris, 1900–1940* (Austin: University of Texas Press, 1986).

Bergonzi, Bernard, *The Myth of Modernism and Twentieth Century Literature* (Brighton: Harvester, 1986).

Borinsky, Alicia, 'Jean Rhys: Poses of a Woman as Guest', in Suleiman, Susan R. (ed.), *The Female Body in Western Culture* (Cambridge and London: Harvard University Press, 1986).

Bowlby, Rachel, *Virginia Woolf: Feminist Destinations* (Oxford: Blackwell, 1988).

Bradbury, Malcolm and James MacFarlane, *Modernism 1890–1930*. (Harmondsworth: Penguin, 1976).

Brathwaite, Edward, *Contradictory Omens* (Mona, Jamaica: Savacour Publications, 1972).

Brooks, Peter, *Reading for the Plot: Design and Intention in Narrative* (Oxford: Clarendon, 1984).

Brown, Nancy Hemond. 'Aspects of the Short Story: A Comparison of Jean Rhys's "The Sound of the River" with Ernest Hemingway's "Hills like White Elephants" ', *Jean Rhys Review*,1,1, 1986, pp.2–12.

Brown, Nancy Hemond, 'On Becoming a Butterfly: Issues of Identity in Jean Rhys's *After Leaving Mr Mackenzie*', *Jean Rhys Review*, 2,1, 1967, pp.6–15.

Campbell, Elaine, 'A Report from Dominica, B.W.I.', *World Literature Written in English*, 17,1, April 1978, pp.305–16.

Campbell, Elaine, Introduction of Virago reprint of Allfrey, Phyllis Shand, *The Orchid House* (London: Virago, 1982).

Campbell, Elaine, 'An Expatriate at Home: Dominica's Elma Napier', *Kunapipi*, 4,1, 1982, pp.82–93.

Campbell, Elaine, 'Reflections of Obeah in Jean Rhys's Fiction', *Kunapipi*, 4,2, 1982, pp.42–50.

Casey, Nancy J., 'The Liberated Woman in Jean Rhys's Later Short Fiction', *Revista Interamericana Review*, 4, 1974, pp.264–72.

Casey, Nancy J., 'Jean Rhys's *Wide Sargasso Sea*', *Revista Interamericana Review*, 4, 1974, pp.340–9.

Chartier, Delphine, 'L'Auto-censure créatrice: Analyse des versions successives de la nouvelle "Rapunzel, Rapunzel" ', *Jean Rhys Review*, 1,1, 1986, pp.15–29.

Clement, Catherine, *Opera; or, The Undoing of Women* (London: Virago, 1989).

Connor, Steven, *Postmodernist Culture: An Introduction to Theories of the Contemporary* (Oxford: Blackwell, 1989).

Cooper, Helen M., Adrienne Munich, and Susan Squier (eds.), *Arms and the Woman: War, Gender, and Literary Representation* (Chapel Hill and London: University of North Carolina Press, 1989).

Coward, Rosalind, *Female Desire* (London: Paladin, 1984).

Coward, Rosalind, 'Are Women's Novels Feminist Novels?' *Feminist Review*, 5, 1980, reprinted in Showalter, Elaine (ed.),*The New Feminist Criticism* (London: Virago, 1986), pp.225–39.

Curtin, Philip D., *The Rise and Fall of the Plantation Complex: Essays in Atlantic History* (Cambridge: Cambridge University Press, 1990).

Dash, Michael, 'In Search of the Lost Body: Redefining the subject in Caribbean Literature', *Kunapipi*, 11,1, 1989, pp.17–26.

Faulkner, Peter, *Modernism* (London and New York: Methuen, 1977).

Fayad, Mona, 'Unquiet Ghosts: The Struggle for Representation in Jean Rhys's *Wide Sargasso Sea*', *Modern Fiction Studies*, 34,3 Autumn 1988, pp.437–52.

Foucault, Michel, 'The Order of Discourse' 1972, reprinted in Young, R. (ed.), *Untying the Text*, (London: Routledge & Kegan Paul, 1981).

Freud, Sigmund, *Complete Psychological Works of Sigmund Freud* (London: Hogarth Standard Edition, 1964).

Gallop, Jane, *The Daughter's Seduction: Feminism and Psychoanalysis* (Ithaca & New York: Cornell University Press, 1982).

Gardiner, Judith Kegan, 'On Female Identity and Writing by Women', in Abel. E. (ed.), *Writing and Sexual Difference* (Brighton: Harvester, 1982).

Gardiner, Judith Kegan, 'Rhys Recalling Ford: *Quartet* and *The Good Soldier*', *Tulsa Studies in Women's Literature*, 1,1, 1982, pp.67–81.

Gilbert, Sandra M. and Susan Gubar, *No Man's Land: The Place of the Woman Writer in the Twentieth Century*. vol.2 (New Haven: Yale University Press, 1989).

Grace, Sherrill, *Regression and Apocalypse: Studies in North American Expressionism* (Toronto and New York: University of Toronto Press, 1989).

Gregg, Veronica Marie, 'Jean Rhys and Modernism: A Different Voice', *Jean Rhys Review*, 1,2, 1987, pp.30–46.

Gubar, Susan, 'The Blank Page and the Issues of Female Creativity', in Abel. E. (ed.), *Writing and Sexual Difference* (Brighton: Harvester, 1982).

Harrison, Nancy R, *Jean Rhys and the Novel as Women's Text* (Chapel Hill and London: University of North Carolina Press, 1988).

Hearne, John, 'The *Wide Sargasso Sea*: A West Indian Reflection', *Cornhill Magazine*, 180, Summer 1974, pp.323–33.

Henke, Suzette A, *James Joyce and the Politics of Desire* (London & New York: Routledge, 1990).

Hochstadt, Pearl, 'From Vulnerability to Selfhood: The Pain-filled Affirmations of Jean Rhys', *Jean Rhys Review*, 2,1, 1987, pp.2–6.

Hollander, Martien Kappers den, 'A Gloomy Child and its Devoted Godmother: *Barred, Sous les Verrous,* and *In der Strik*' in MacDermott, Doreann (ed.), *Autobiographical and Biographical Writing in the Commonwealth* (Barcelona: Editorial AUSA, 1984).

Hollander, Martien Kappers den, 'Measure for Measure: *Quartet* and *When the Wicked Man*', *Jean Rhys Review*, 2,2, 1988, pp.2–17.

Howells, Robin J., *Carnival to Classicism: The Comic Novels of Charles Sorel* (Paris, Seattle, Tubingen: Biblio 17, 1989).

Hutcheon, Linda, *A Poetics of Postmodernism: History, Theory, Fiction* (New York & London: Routledge, 1988).

Hutcheon, Linda, *The Canadian Postmodern: Studies in Contemporary English Canadian Fiction* (Oxford: OUP, 1988).

Huyssen, Andreas, *After the Great Divide: Modernism, Mass Culture, Postmodernism* (Bloomington: Indiana University Press, 1986).

James, Louis, *Jean Rhys*. (London: Longman, 1978).

James, Selma, *The Ladies and the Mammies: Jane Austen and Jean Rhys* (Bristol: Falling Wall Press, 1983).

Jameson, Fredric, 'Magical Narratives: Romance as Genre', *New Literary History*, 7,1, 1975, pp.135–59.

Jardine, Alice, *Gynesis: Configurations of Woman and Modernity* (Ithaca and London: Cornell University Press, 1985).

Juhasz, Suzanne, (ed.), *Feminist Critics Read Emily Dickinson* (Bloomington: Indiana University Press, 1983).

Kloepfer, Deborah Kelly, *The Unspeakable Mother: Forbidden Discourse in Jean Rhys and H.D.* (Ithaca and London: Cornell University Press, 1989).

Knight, Franklin W., *The Caribbean: The Genesis of a Fragmented Nationalism* (New York: OUP, 1978).

Leigh, Nancy J., 'Mirror Mirror: The Development of Female Identity in Jean Rhys's Fiction', *World Literature Written in English*, 25,2, 1985, pp.270–85.

Lewis, Gordon K., *Main Currents in Caribbean Thought: The Historical Evolution of Caribbean Society in its Ideological Aspects, 1492–1900* (Baltimore: Johns Hopkins University Press, 1983).

Lodge, David, *The Modes of Modern Writing* (London: Arnold, 1977).

Look Lai, Wally, 'The Road to Thornfield Hall. A Review of *Wide Sargasso Sea*', *New Beacon Reviews*, 1968, pp.38–52.

Ludwig, R.M. (ed.), *Letters of Ford Madox Ford* (Princeton: Princeton University Press, 1965).

Marks, Elaine and Isabelle de Courtivron (eds.), *New French Feminisms: An Anthology* (Brighton: Harvester, 1980).

Mellown, Elgin W., *Jean Rhys: A Descriptive and Annotated Bibliography of Works and Criticism* (New York and London: Gale, 1984).

Miller, Nancy K., 'Emphasis Added: Plots and Plausibilities in Women's Fiction', reprinted in Showalter. E. (ed), *The New Feminist Criticism* (London: Virago, 1986).

Mintz, Sidney W. and Sally Price, *Caribbean Contours* (Baltimore and London: Johns Hopkins University Press, 1985).

Mitchell, Juliet, 'Femininity, Narrative, and Psychoanalysis', reprinted in Lodge, David (ed.), *Modern Criticism and Theory: A Reader* (London and New York: Longman, 1988).

Moi, Toril, *Sexual/Textual Politics* (London: Methuen, 1985).

Munro, Alice, *The Moons of Jupiter.* (Toronto: Macmillan, 1982).

Naipaul, V.S., 'Without a Dog's Chance', *New York Review of Books*, 18 May 1972, p.29.

Nebeker, Helen., *Jean Rhys, Woman in Passage: A Critical Study* (Montreal : Eden Press, 1981).

O'Connor, Teresa F., *Jean Rhys's West Indian Novels* (New York and London: New York University Press, 1986).

Petersen, Kirstin Holst and Anna Rutherford (eds.), *A Double Colonisation: Colonial and Post-Colonial Women's Writing* (Aarhus: Dangaroo Press, 1986).

Plante, David, 'Jean Rhys: A Remembrance', *Paris Review*, 76, 1979, pp.238-58.

Plante, David, *Difficult Women: A Memoir of Three* (London: Gollancz, 1983).

Du Plessis, Rachel Blau, *Writing Beyond the Ending: Narrative Strategies of Twentieth-Century Women Writers* (Bloomington: Indiana University Press, 1985).

Ramchand, Kenneth, *The West Indian Novel and Its Background* (London: Heinemann, 1970).

Roe, Sue, 'The Shadow of Light: The Symbolic Underworld of Jean Rhys', in Roe, Sue (ed.), *Women Reading Women's Writing* (Brighton: Harvester, 1987).

Russo, Mary, 'Female Grotesques: Carnival and Theory', in Laurentis, Teresa de (ed.), *Feminist Studies/Critical Studies* (Bloomington: Indiana University Press, 1986).

Scott, Bonnie Kime (ed.), *The Gender of Modernism: A Critical Anthology* (Bloomington and Indianapolis: Indiana University Press, 1990).

Sedgwick, Eve Kosofsky, *The Coherence of Gothic Conventions* (New York and London: Methuen, 1986).

Slemon, Stephen, 'Monuments of Empire: Allegory, Counter-Discourse, Post-Colonial Writing', *Kunapipi*, 9,3, 1987, pp.1–16.

Snitow, Ann, 'Mass Market Romance: Pornography for women is different', in Snitow, A., C. Stansell, and S. Thompson (eds.), *Desire: The Politics of Sexuality* (London: Virago, 1984).

Spivak, Gayatri Chakravorty, 'Three Women's Texts and a Critique of Imperialism', *Critical Inquiry*, 12, Autumn 1985, pp.243–61.

Squier, Susan Merrill, *Virginia Woolf and London: Sexual Politics of the City* (Chapel Hill and London: University of North Carolina Press, 1985).
Squier, Susan Merrill, 'Virginia Woolf's London and the Feminist Revision of Modernism', to appear in Caws, Mary Ann (ed.), *City, Text, Thought* (New York: Gordon and Breach Science Publishers, forthcoming).
Staley, Thomas F., *Jean Rhys: A Critical Study* (London: Macmillan, 1979).
Stead, C.K., *Pound, Yeats, Eliot and the Modernist Movement* (London: Macmillan, 1985).
Symons, Julian, *Makers of the New: The Revolution in Literature, 1912-1939* (London: Deutsch, 1987).
Thieme, John, 'Apparitions of Disaster: Brontëan Parallels in *Wide Sargasso Sea* and *Guerillas*', *Journal of Commonwealth Literature*, 14,1, 1979, pp.116–32.
Tiffin, Helen, 'Post-Colonial Literatures and Counter-Discourses', *Kunapipi*, 9,3, 1987, pp.17–34.
Tiffin, Helen, 'Mirror and Mask: Colonial Motifs in the Novels of Jean Rhys', *World Literature Written in English*, 17, 1978 pp.328–41.
Vreeland, Elizabeth, 'Jean Rhys: The Art of Fiction LXIV', *Paris Review*, 76, 1979, pp.291-317.
Waugh, Alec, *The Sugar Islands* (London: Cassell, 1958).
Williams, Eric, *From Columbus to Castro: The History of the Caribbean, 1492–1969* (London: Andre Deutsch, 1970).
Wilson, Lucy, ' "Women Must Have Spunks": Jean Rhys's West Indian Outcasts', *Modern Fiction Studies*, 32,3, Autumn 1986, pp.439–48.
Young, Robert (ed.), *Untying the Text: A Post-Structuralist Reader* (Boston and London: Routledge & Kegan Paul, 1981).

# *Index*